To Brianne!
You can give me
a massage any
time

xoxo

Allan

13

13

A Leap From the Method

An Organic Approach to Acting

by
Allan Rich

Bloomington, IN Milton Keynes, UK

authorHOUSE®

AuthorHouse™
1663 Liberty Drive,
Suite 200
Bloomington, IN 47403
www.authorhouse.com
Phone: 1-800-839-8640

AuthorHouse™ UK Ltd.
500 Avebury Boulevard
Central Milton Keynes,
MK9 2BE
www.authorhouse.co.uk
Phone: 08001974150

First published by AuthorHouse   1/8/2007

ISBN: 978-1-4208-2223-6 (sc)

Library of Congress Control Number: 2005902704

Printed in the United States of America
Bloomington, Indiana

This book is printed on acid-free paper.

To Elaine, my wife of 56 years,
who made all this possible.
This book is dedicated to her.

TABLE OF CONTENTS

PREFACE

When Allan Rich asked me to edit this book, I was intrigued by the prospect of learning more about the craft of acting. As a writer with experience in film and theater, I looked forward to getting the inside scoop on the actor's process. I found Allan's technique to be sensible, insightful, and, above all, liberating for the actor. There were no cryptic terms or vague directives, just simple common sense tempered by his many years of putting the technique to work in his own acting career.

What impressed me most, however, was that Allan's teaching treats the actor as a whole person. Unlike most acting coaches, Allan understands that no one lives or works in a vacuum and that growing in the *craft* of acting means growing in the *art* of living. His ideas about education, success, and psychology made enormous sense to me as a writer and a person.

What I realized during the process of editing this book is that it is not just about acting and not just for actors. The ideas contained herein can be just as applicable to the salesman, the politician, or the physician as they are to the performer. The ideas in this book can be applied to anyone who deals with the public or who must present him or herself to other people. *A Leap from the Method* can also be most useful to anyone who is pursuing any creative field. Inhibition isn't just experienced by actors.

The best example of the profound effect the ideas in this book can have beyond the scope of acting is Allan's work with a young actor named Peter Antico. Of all his many students (including stars such as Sharon Stone, Rene Russo, Jamie Lee Curtis, Larry Miller, and Alan Thicke), Allan is most proud of his work with Peter. He came to Allan like many young actors looking to improve his work, except that Peter had the additional challenge of having Tourette's Syndrome. Tourette's is a neurological disorder that causes its sufferers to experience shaking, facial tics, uncontrollable urges, and verbal outbursts of obscene language. After learning the techniques found in this book during five years of study with Allan, Peter learned focus and concentration (two important skills for an actor). His confidence soared and he was able to gain control of his Tourette's. He has virtually conquered this difficult disorder, and its effects are no longer outwardly noticeable [when acting].

Peter has gone on to have a flourishing career in television and film, appearing in movies like *Lethal Weapon III, 29th Street, Jurassic Park II,* and fifteen other films and numerous television shows.

What Peter Antico proves is that this book can be enormously helpful for anyone looking to overcome inhibition and develop self-confidence. If you wish to present yourself publicly in a confident, self-assured manner, there are many useful ideas here.

Robert Kernen, 1996

(Mr. Kernen was the original editor of *A Leap from the Method* before it was rewritten and edited in 2006.)

Former student and working actor, Peter Antico

CHAPTER 1
A PERSONAL OUTLINE

Most people who call themselves actors are merely relying on inspiration or luck to see them through the day. They are "acting by accident." They go through the motions, saddled by the insecurity and doubt of not having a reference, procedure, gauge, or standard with which to guide their work. In all the arts and professions, confidence comes from mastering your craft.

To share what I've learned during my sixty-five years in the acting profession is what I love to do. I'm an eighty-year-old actor still striving to land my next job. Every day, I experience the same problems and challenges as any other actor. I offer my story as an example of just how difficult, joyous, hurtful, and exciting it can be to pursue a career in this crazy business.

I don't offer my career as a yardstick by which to measure your own or anyone else's. There are as many different career paths as there are actors. Consider where you began, where you are now, and where you wish to go. I hope my experience will tune you in to the best acting classroom of all: your own life and the world around you.

I was born Benjamin Norman Schultz in 1926. My mother, Ella, kept telling the following story to anyone who'd listen: "I spent my last dollar and took little Benji to a movie and a vaudeville show for his third birthday." That's how she'd always begin. "Suddenly, my Benji jumped out of his seat, ran onto the stage, and began to sing

'Ain't She Sweet.' He's a real actor, a little Eddie Cantor." She was proud of me. She thought I was a natural, a real actor!

Now that I think of it, I realize my mother was projecting her own desire to act onto me. She was a regular drama queen, Ella was, a stay-at-home actress who loved to make mountains out of molehills.

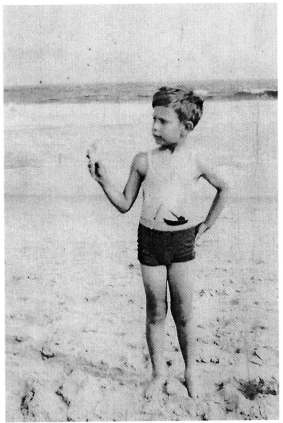

Is it possible that I was playing Hamlet at 6 years old? "Alas, poor Yorick!"

Like the time my grandmother overfed our goldfish to death. Concerned that I would seriously mourn its passing, Ella actually arranged a funeral. We all gathered around the toilet as she said the Hebrew prayer for the dead. Then she flushed that fat dead fish down the bowl. As she pulled the chain, she said, "He's now in fishy heaven." Did she think I would believe that the path to heaven was through the toilet bowl? No wonder I became an atheist.

In the bath one night, some crazy idea came over my six-year-old brain. I decided to float face down in the tub and hold my breath. I can't remember why, but I wanted to see if I could fool Ella into believing I was dead.

Soon, I heard Ella's blood-curdling scream. "Benji, are you alright?!" I picked my head up out of the water and sang, "ta-dah!" She slapped the smile right off my face. "When you were an infant and couldn't catch your breath, I walked the floors with you," she screamed at me. "Doctor Herzog gave up on your asthma, but I didn't!" Dr. Herzog had treated me for asthma when I was two years old.

Ella shook me until I finally gasped, "I'm sorry, I'll never do it again. Please don't tell Pop." I pleaded with her until she swore she'd never tell. Nevertheless, she told him anyway.

I was reared by two confused parents—Ella and Arnold Schultz. They never planned anything. Not me. Not my younger brother, Kenny. They lived and died without ever knowing what happened in-between.

Like so many families during the Great Depression, they struggled endlessly just to keep afloat. Pop sold tomatoes off a truck. He worked nights and slept in all day. I only saw him on Sundays. In exchange for rent, Ella was the superintendent of our two-family house. She stoked coals in the basement while Arnold slept.

Ella the drama queen just couldn't keep from telling Arnold how much aggravation I caused her every day. But not Kenny, her sweet little angel. He was always the good one. I was always the bad one.

Most Sundays, after Ella had given Arnold an earful, he'd say, "Assume the angle." I'd lean on my bed and stick my ass out. He enjoyed belting me with that strap of his. Ten whacks, I'd get. His whippings were never hard enough to make me bleed or anything; still, they were bad enough to keep me hating him for years and years.

My earliest memories are of our house in Astoria, Queens, just a short distance from Manhattan. Our neighborhood was predominantly Greek. When I was six, one of my playmates said, "My mudder told me that you killed Christ."

I replied, "Me? I didn't even know him." I didn't have a clue what he was talking about, but when I repeated the encounter to my parents, they sure did.

We were the only Jews on our block in Astoria. Anti-Semitism was everywhere around us. At first, I didn't really understand it, but I knew that it made me feel different and alone. Ella and Arnold must have felt the same, because in 1933 we moved to Sheridan Avenue, a Jewish neighborhood in the West Bronx, just north of Manhattan.

We now lived smack in the middle of the biggest melting pot the world has ever known. This new part of New York was completely different from small-town Astoria. We had moved from a tiny neighborhood of Greeks in little one-family houses to a big world of six-story apartment buildings. Each street housed a different ethnic group: Irish, Jewish, German, Italian, Polish, Russian, black.

With all the drama that went on in that multinational neighborhood, I couldn't have landed in a better place to instinctively start to become an actor. At school,

I heard all the dialects. Soon I could mimic a lot of them. In addition, after a few beatings, I learned how to fight. You had to, because each block had its own gang. These weren't like contemporary gangs—no guns, just fists, sticks, stones, and spit.

In the third grade, I played a mouse in the school play. I was given a set of big ears and a tail to wear and I loved it. I got big laughs. Boy, was I hooked.

My fifth-grade teacher, Miss Jean Steigman, was the great catalyst of my young life. She tried to read _Julius Caesar_ to our class of ethnic rowdies but couldn't get through the first scene. I didn't like the way my buddies catcalled and made jokes. I liked the way she read the story and wanted to hear more. I somehow got up the courage to ask Miss Steigman to read it to me after school. She did, and we remained friends for the rest of her long life.

After that experience, I really began to resent poor Ella and Arnold. Why was I stuck with those two? I used to daydream that Miss Steigman could adopt me. I was sure she loved me. She cast me in all of the school plays.

In my final year of grammar school, when I was thirteen, I played Ko-Ko in Gilbert and Sullivan's _The Mikado_ and received the Dramatic Medal at graduation. I thought my folks would be proud, but instead Ella just kept reminding me that while she'd come to all my plays, Arnold had always claimed he had to sleep. I think he was just jealous.

After graduation, Miss Steigman recommended Norman Brace's Dramatic School at Carnegie Hall in Manhattan so I could improve my Bronx speech. Ella and Arnold said no, but I insisted. I refused to go to school until—miraculously—they finally gave in.

I soon began taking the subway into the City every Sunday morning. Though the classes cost two dollars a week, I knew Arnold could afford it now. We had recently moved into a bigger apartment on the Grand Concourse, a much ritzier section of the Bronx. It was 1939 and he was finally making some good money selling repackaged tomatoes to the U.S. Army.

Every Saturday I went to the movies at the Luxor Theatre on 170th Street with my best friend, Sid Maurer. (Even after seventy years, Sid is still an integral part of my life. He did the artwork for the front cover of this book.) Those afternoon movies were the great escape of our young lives.

I saw all the great films of the 1930s and early 1940s: *Little Caesar,* with Edward G. Robinson; *The Good Earth* and *Scarface,* both starring Paul Muni; *Lost Horizon,* with Sam Jaffe; *City for Conquest,* starring Jimmy Cagney; and *Grapes of Wrath,* with Henry Fonda. Sitting there in the dark, I knew what I wanted to be—a movie actor. I constantly dreamed about being up there on the big screen. Little did I know, years later I'd wind up working with many of my childhood idols.

From age thirteen to fifteen, I continued to study speech and movement at Norman Brace's during the school year. Over the long break, Norman ran a summer stock company in Lake Bomoseen, Vermont. When I was fifteen, he cast me as Henry Aldrich (a then-famous role) in Clifford Goldsmith's *What a Life.*

Even though I played the lead role, there was no pay. I was a summer apprentice but I didn't care. That apprenticeship meant I could spend nearly three months away from home.

Norman Brace had promised me feature billing on the poster. Upon my arrival, though, he changed his mind. We weren't in New York anymore. This was Vermont. They didn't know from Schultzes, Schwartzes, or Goldbergs. "I can't have 'Benjamin Norman Schultz as Henry Aldrich' on my poster," he explained. "You'll have to change your name."

A production still from *What a Life* in 1943

I was devastated. I had told Ella, Arnold, and all my friends about my billing. I was looking forward to bringing one of those posters home with me. What to do?

Monday through Wednesday, the theater became a dance hall with a live band. Dancing with the ingénue from the play one evening, I tried to tell her that Norman was making me change my name. We were dancing in front of the bandstand where I had to shout so she could hear me over the music. Wouldn't you know it, the bandleader heard my sad words. He leaned down and in a loud whisper said, "I just changed my name to Devlin Blake. You're welcome to use my old stage name—Allan Rich."

I gleefully looked up and said, "I'll take it!" Forever after, I've used that orchestra leader's discarded name.

That summer I also had bit parts in Sidney Howard's *They Knew What They Wanted* and George S. Kaufman's *You Can't Take It With You.* I then stage-managed Emlyn Williams' *Night Must Fall,* a murder mystery. Every night of the run, I stood in the wings hoping someday I'd have the chance to play a great role like Danny the Hatbox Murderer. I really understood who he was. I had grown up with guys just like him. Danny was raised poor. He worked as a waiter and hated all the rich and snotty women who gave him orders.

This is my daughter Marian playing Harpo Marx with the signature wig and hat.

The last production of the summer was Kaufman's *The Man Who Came to Dinner,* a very funny play with great roles. On opening night, the actor who played the part of Banjo was too sick to go on. They put Harpo Marx makeup on me and I played Banjo after only one rehearsal. I didn't miss a line. What a hoot! I've never forgotten that summer in Vermont.

Back home, our family finances may have been in better shape, but my mid-teens were still hellish. The Japanese had bombed Pearl Harbor and World War II had begun for the U.S. Meanwhile, I was conducting my own private war.

I was no longer a cute, funny kid. In fact, I was becoming downright ugly. I was sprouting elephant-like ears. My nose and lips looked too big for my face. Other kids would see me and say things like "Here comes blubber lips," or "Wow! What a schnozz!"

By the time I was nearly seventeen I couldn't take it anymore. I'd read somewhere about local doctors working miracles with the wounded soldiers who were sent home needing their faces fixed. I told Ella and Arnold that I wouldn't leave the house until they paid someone to have *my* face fixed.

I wasn't going to go through life with girls laughing at me. My friend Trudy had tried to set me up on a date with a girl at school but she'd turned me down. I heard later that she'd called me an ugly mutt. I hated her but I hated myself more.

I gave Ella and Arnold every argument in the book. Without some help, I'd go through life the butt of people's jokes. How could I seriously pursue my career as an actor? No one was going to pay good money to see my ugly mug. I needed help and I needed it fast. Arnold even brought home a little bull terrier we named Chubby as a way to placate me, but I still insisted on getting my nose fixed.

Finally, they gave in. Pop found a top-notch plastic surgeon, Dr. John Cinnelli. He agreed to fix my nose for $700. By that time, Arnold was supplying the whole U.S. Army with tomatoes, so he sprang for the $700—a large sum in those days. In retrospect, I understand how lucky I was to have such caring parents.

As Dr. Cinnelli prepared to operate, he studied my whole face. His words were music to my extra-large ears: "Benjamin, if I only do your nose, it won't fit the rest of your face. So for the same price I'll do your lips and ears too." He was a great surgeon. He fixed my face and changed my life forever.

In early 1943, I turned seventeen. Most days after school, I would go directly home, drop off my books, and get ready to make the rounds. I rushed to get onto the subway to Times Square. The newsstands there carried *Actors Cues,* a mimeographed sheet listing the agents and producers currently casting productions on Broadway and on the road. It was a valuable precursor to *Backstage* and *Dramalogue.*

In those days, it was easy to make the rounds. The Broadway theater scene was wide open. You could walk into a production office or casting agency and ask, "Is there anything today?" and maybe they would say: "Yes, we are doing a play, you're right for the part." Or, more likely: "Sorry, nothing today."

Among the many places I checked out regularly was Arthur Hopkins Productions. "Hoppy" was a famous producer responsible for many Broadway plays in the 1920s and 1930s. He ran a busy production office on West 44th Street.

One day, in the spring of 1943, I visited Hoppy's place only to find the hallway outside his office full of young guys waiting to audition for someone in the office next door. I heard they were looking for an actor to play the bratty kid brother, Raymond, in a play called *I'll Take the High Road.* I joined the rest of the actors waiting to read. Jimmy Russo, the stage manager, emerged every few minutes to call us in, one by one.

I waited around until they finally called me. When I entered the inner office, I saw

Me with my dear friend Milton Berle

a very familiar looking man sitting on the desk, chewing on the last little nub of a cigar. After a moment, I recognized him from the movies: It was Milton Berle. Sitting behind the desk looking like a college professor was Berle's co-producer, Clifford Hayman. They asked me if I wanted to read and I said, "Yeah, sure. When?"

They set up an appointment for a few weeks later. Just then, Milton Berle threw his wet and disgusting cigar remnant out the window. Then a voice from the street yelled out, "Hey mister, you dropped your cigar!" The kid down below had an unusually squeaky voice that caused both Berle and Hayman to chuckle.

Milton Berle looked out the window and said, "Hey you, young man, do you want to be an actor?"

"No," the fellow squeaked out in response, "You dropped your cigar!" This time they laughed heartily. I did too.

Milton told him to come up to the third floor. "I think we can use you in the last act!" he shouted down to the street. I stood there receiving no attention. It was as if I suddenly didn't exist.

A moment later, the guy walked in, cigar in hand. "Get this guy a contract," Milton said to Hayman. "You are now an actor," he pronounced to his new recruit, the slightly bewildered Gordon Hammill. He was cast in the play and I was sent home. (As far as I know, that was Gordon Hammill's only acting job.)

I had the chance to read for Milton and Clifford a few weeks later. They were still casting *I'll Take the High Road,* and though I thought my audition went well, I waited weeks and never heard anything.

It was nearly the end of August, right before I was to begin my senior year in high school, and still no word. One particularly hot night, I was home bored out of my mind, trying not to stick to Ella's plastic-covered couch while she played mahjong with her girlfriends in the living room. Simultaneously, Pop played gin rummy with his buddies in the kitchen. The phone rang right next to Arnold. He picked it up, then yelled, "Benji, it's for Allan Rich."

I almost swallowed my tongue. I ran into the kitchen and grabbed the phone. The voice on the phone said, "So you want to be an actor?" It was Mr. Hayman.

"Yes," I yelled. He told me to come to rehearsal with one of my parents so they could sign the contracts, and that was that. I was now a professional actor on Broadway at the age of seventeen. If I hadn't made the rounds that day and gone to Hoppy's office, I never would've known about the audition next door, and I never would have gotten that phone call weeks later. I was in the right place at the right time. While vigorously pursuing your career, you can never know where the next job is coming from, but if you sit at home waiting for the phone to ring, you may never work at all.

At this point, many boys my age were joining or being drafted into the armed forces. I wasn't eligible to serve because I had been declared 4F because of my asthma. Even when I turned 18, I couldn't be drafted.

Former Group Theater member Sanford Meisner directed *I'll Take the High Road,* but I don't remember being directed by him. In our last week of rehearsal, Milton Berle unexpectedly replaced Meisner as director. I have no idea why.

On opening night, my father bought tickets so all his cronies could see his son, the Broadway actor. After the play, Arnold "Big Shot" Schultz treated his whole group to a great dinner at Sardi's Restaurant on West 44th Street. Could it be that my father was finally proud of me? (Years later I wrote a screenplay about Arnold called *The Tomato King.*)

I received a nice review, but the play did not. The *New York Post* wrote: "I'll Take the High Road runs hither and yon, but nowhere." I wondered years later if that job

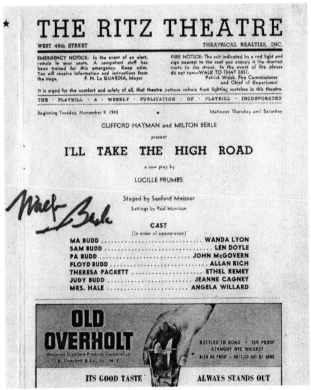

**The playbill for *I'll Take The High Road,*
autographed by Milton Berle, September 1943.**

typecast me for a while. I kept being cast in bratty kid roles. I liked playing those parts because they weren't far from my own wise-guy personality.

Shortly after my opening night triumph, I had my first professional disappointment—the play closed after only five performances. Though there were only three people in the audience at the final matinee, all the actors performed as if we had a full house. Even if there is only one person in the audience, you owe that one patron your best performance.

The upside of *I'll Take the High Road* was my lifelong relationships with Milton Berle and Clifford Hayman. Both men opened doors, arranged readings, and mentored me in many ways for many years.

After closing night, Arnold informed me that since I had dropped out of school to be a full-time actor, I had better get a job. And I did. Clifford Hayman made a couple of calls on my behalf and I was lucky enough to be cast in a new Broadway play, *Bright Boy*—yet another snotty wise-ass. Produced by David Merrick, the play starred a fine English actor, Ivan Simpson.

I was flying high—two Broadway shows in one season. I felt invincible. And full of myself. I floated around the neighborhood like a big, hot-air balloon just waiting to be popped.

Rehearsal was four weeks, but you could be fired at any time within the first five days. As per the Equity contract, after five days the producers have to pay the actor for the entire run of the play. Sure enough, I was fired at the very end of the fifth day. Mr. Merrick said they had rewritten my part for two small boys. I was obsessed with the incident. In my head, I went over every little detail of what Merrick had said. What had I done to get fired? Had I said something wrong? Maybe the cast didn't like me. Maybe Merrick was just trying to let me down easy? I tossed and turned all night.

Being fired is every actor's worst nightmare. It doesn't make you a failure, though—or a bad actor—it just makes life inconsolable for a few days. In my case, however, I got up the next morning, dressed, had breakfast, and told Ella that I'd get another Broadway show.

Off to the D train I went, down to 42nd and Broadway. I got a copy of *Actors Cues* and saw: "Career Angel: director Don Appell is seeing young people at 1501 Broadway." I scooted over there as fast as I could.

The office was already crowded with guys my age. I waited hours for my turn. Once in Appell's office, I gave an energetic cold reading. Looking him square in the eye, I said, "I'm the best young actor in this town." I must have said it with total conviction because he hired me on the spot. I played the lead kid in an orphanage.

The play starred Glen Anders and Whitford Kane, two famous Broadway stars of the period. We spent a week in Boston at the Wilbur Theater, and then opened on Broadway at the National Theater. But alas, we closed three weeks later. It was another short run, but at least it was longer than five days and much better than being fired.

Nineteen forty-four to 1945 was a banner time for me. In addition to Broadway, I did two more road shows, and then, in the spring of 1945 at age nineteen, I read for the coveted role of Henry Aldrich in the USO production of Clifford Goldsmith's *What a Life.* Since I'd already played Henry a few summers before, I nailed the audition and won the part. The author directed the production.

The idea of entertaining the troops overseas really appealed to me. Even though I was 4F, I was eager to be a part of the war in whatever way I could. After a month of rehearsal in New York, the cast was issued khaki uniforms and we shipped out. I thought we had it made! Although we remained civilians, we were equal in rank to captains as company grade officers. Plus the pay was a generous $150 per week, banked in our names back home because the USO paid all our expenses.

Twenty-two days after boarding a huge troop ship in San Francisco, we were sweltering in the jungles of New Guinea. Island hopping via large twin-engine C-47 transport aircraft, we performed on makeshift stages, in mess halls, and off the backs of trucks. We provided much-needed entertainment. Many of the GIs had not seen home for thirty-six months. Entire regiments, who'd fought from island to island, had been nearly wiped out.

Through April, May, and the start of June of 1945, I was sleeping under mosquito nets, eating GI food, and swallowing Atabrine and salt tablets to prevent malaria and dehydration. We performed every afternoon and evening in extreme heat and humidity. During a show one night in June, several Japanese planes bombed us. Everyone scattered. I jumped off the stage and landed flat on my stomach. Soon the all-clear sounded. A few feet from me, a GI had been hit. He shrieked with pain. The medics placed him on a stretcher. I was sick to my stomach.

A week later, I passed out after a show. They flew me to the 55th station hospital in Finchhaven, New Guinea. I had contracted a serious form of bacillary and amoebic dysentery. I was so sick for a while I couldn't keep anything down and lost weight rapidly. In no time at all, I'd lost eighty pounds.

After a few weeks rest, I begged the doctors to get me to my USO unit on the island of Tacloban in the Philippines. Somehow, they found a way to fly me there, and I happily rejoined my fellow actors. After performing that first night back, though, I once again passed out after the show.

This time I was sent to Manila to recuperate. My doctors there thought my condition was serious enough to send me back to the U.S. I was staying in an officer's billet

My dog, Chubby

waiting for a ship back home when I heard the news about the atomic bombs and the end of the war in the Pacific. I later found out my USO unit had continued to war-torn Tokyo, another disappointment. I would have done anything to return to the company and perform for our troops in Japan.

Not long after hearing about the Japanese surrender, I was finally on a troop ship bound for San Francisco. Those servicemen partied all the way home. The war was over. The USO took great care of me and continued to support me through the many months of my recovery.

When I arrived back at 730 Grand Concourse, my little dog, Chubby, leapt into my arms from ten feet way. I was even happy to see Ella and Arnold, and especially my brother, Kenny; he was always my biggest fan. They flew me to Miami for a long holiday and to fatten me up. The USO arranged and paid for the dysentery shots I had to endure for the next year and a half.

During the long months of my recuperation, that generous $150 per week check kept coming from the USO, and I kept smoking, drinking, and carousing with the girls, making the foolish mistakes of a twenty-year-old. The thought of restarting my acting career gave me acute anxiety. My champions had left town. Cliff Hayman had gone to Hollywood to work as a casting director and Milton Berle was away somewhere, probably on vacation or on the road with his vaudeville act. I felt abandoned, worried, depressed and angry—a total mess.

My brother and biggest fan, Kenny Schultz

In late 1945, I convinced an old classmate, Stan Burns, a discontented disk jockey at WINS in New York, to move out West with me so we could seek our fortunes in Hollywood. He owned a car and off we drove to Los Angeles, where I had arranged to camp with my Aunt Helen.

Stan immediately picked up a radio job, and I joined a local community theater in Hollywood. I soon discovered, though, that I had somehow lost all my acting talent. What had earlier come to me automatically stopped coming at all. I had been on Broadway and now I couldn't even handle roles in a small-time community theater! I don't remember whether they let me go or I quit, but in any event, I panicked. Inhibition had reared its ugly head and I was in its throes.

Months of hand-wringing followed. I didn't return Cliff Hayman's calls. If he arranged a reading for me, I found excuses not to show. I was sure I would fail. Fortunately, for me, a few months after our arrival, Stan called to say he'd been offered his old job back with a big pay raise. At that point, I was anxious to return to New York. Maybe I'd do better back home. We packed up and immediately drove back to the Big Apple.

Inhibition is a problem that plagues every actor at some point in his or her career. For me acting was fine while I was in my teens; the talent seemed to pour out of me like a childlike gift. In my early twenties, though, out of work and frightened, I no longer trusted my instincts. I began to second-guess my meager training at Norman Brace's Academy. Inhibitions are closely linked to the universal actor's disease, "I gotta be good." As long as I was obsessed with "I gotta be good," my performances suffered and I was acting by accident.

Panicked as I was, for the first time I made a conscious decision to study and learn about acting. I read Stanislavsky's classic *An Actor Prepares.* Much of it went over my head. What does he mean by "the magic If," "the creative mood," or "the given circumstances"? What are the "actions," or "the kernel of a play?" Many of these things confused me.

As I asked around, I heard and read stories about the Group Theater and their teachings based on Stanislavsky's Method. In the early 1930s the Group Theater

Morris Carnovsky (1897–1992).
Artwork by Sid Maurer.

productions of plays like Sidney Kingsley's *Men in White* (the first real hospital drama), and *Waiting for Lefty* by Clifford Odets dynamically broke ranks with the stereotypical melodramas of the day. These productions touched audiences in emotional ways that they'd never previously experienced in the theater.

After sitting in on various acting classes, I was lucky enough to find and be accepted into a great scene class led by two of the best acting coaches around—former Group Theater members Morris Carnovsky and J. Edward (Joe) Bromberg. Morris and Joe taught their students through kindness and love. Suddenly they began to make some sense of "the magic if" and the "given circumstances." As I understood it, "the magic If" went something like this:

If I were the character, how would I behave? When I played the Taxi Driver in a scene from Clifford Odets' **Waiting for Lefty,** I said to myself, "*If* I were that taxi driver from New York, how would I speak and dress? How would I act *if* I were constantly being nagged by my wife because I couldn't bring home enough money to support the family?"

As for the "given circumstances," Morris and Joe defined those as everything the author gives you that is happening in the scene. For the Taxi Driver, his "givens" were constant bickering, living in dire poverty, tattered clothing, a strike looming, and pressure from within and without in the midst of the Great Depression. With all the above things subtly helping me work towards my goal of becoming the Taxi Driver, I almost unconsciously played him full of nervous energy, and I reverted back to the "dese, dems, and dose"s of my childhood.

The more I listened to Morris and Joe's critiques of our scene work, the more I realized they were trying to lead us back to the same instincts that had worked for me as a teenager. The goal seemed the same—the actor must immerse himself or herself in an invented reality in order to become the character. I thought I was learning to create that new reality, but over time it became clearer and clearer that something was still missing; each scene still felt somehow incomplete. I knew there was much more to do, but I didn't know where it was or how to find it at that moment.

Joe Bromberg (1903–1951). *Artwork by Sid Maurer*

I continued to have serious doubts, which I eventually expressed to Joe. "Allan, work, don't worry," he counseled in response. From then on, every time I felt those doubts, I'd say to myself, "Work, don't worry," keeping Joe Bromberg on my shoulder. Hearing his soothing voice in my head pushed me to work like a demon. I rehearsed my scenes with my partners over and over again, scene after scene, until I slowly began to overcome some of my inhibitions and gain a bit of confidence.

In any event, I loved what I was doing. Because of Joe I was open to learning more and more. I remember one time when Joe gave me the perfect bit of direction to help me find the key to playing a convincing love scene opposite a gal I couldn't even manage to feign interest in, let alone feel anything close to love. Joe took me aside and said, "Allan, think of her as the girl you always wished to have." Looking at my scene partner, I worked with what Joe had told me. I imagined that she was my dream girl. I imagined she looked like Rita Hayworth: flowing red hair, kissable red lips, and a figure that wouldn't quit. All this fantasizing transformed her into my idealized sexual partner. Wow! Suddenly the scene became alive (and so did I).

Cliff Hayman eventually returned from the Coast, and lo and behold, he landed me an agent, Lucille Phillips. She began sending me out on auditions, and I soon won a role in the road company of *Pickup Girl,* playing, you guessed it, a young wise guy. The show starred Peggy Ann Garner, who had been widely acclaimed as the young girl in Elia Kazan's film *A Tree Grows in Brooklyn.*

"Allan Rich plays his role way beyond his years," read my mention in *Pickup Girl*'s positive review in the *Philadelphia Inquirer.* It was a real confidence booster!

Late in the spring of 1946, after six weeks on the road, *Pickup Girl* closed in Toledo, Ohio. Coincidentally, my childhood friend Ed Fisher, just out of the Army, was attending Antioch College in Yellow Springs, Ohio, on the G.I. Bill.

Ed had influenced me hugely as a kid. He was the most cultured guy I'd ever met. Without him, I wouldn't have known about (and loved) art, classical music, great literature. In a sense, he taught me how to think. Ed became a great political cartoonist, and his work was featured in the *New Yorker* magazine for over forty years.

That's me in the back row, third from the right; Ed Fisher, second from right. Ed played Pooh-Bah to my Ko-Ko in our school play *The Mikado* in 1939.

Since it wasn't far from Toledo, I used part of my last ninety dollars to take the bus to Yellow Springs to visit my old friend. I hadn't seen him since he'd been drafted nearly two years before. I ended up staying at Antioch for three years.

Antioch College leased an old opera house and supported a community theater called the Area Theater. They did twenty plays a year: ten in the summer and ten in the winter, mostly classics. Ed introduced me to Professor Paul Treichler, the Creative Director and head of the Theater Arts Department at Antioch. Mr. Treichler took a liking to me and allowed me to join the college's theater company even though I wasn't a student.

I loved being at Antioch. I met all the professors and many of the citizens of Yellow Springs who supported the Area Theater. It seemed the whole region surrounding the college was involved with theater. We played to full houses all the time. Our work was respected and appreciated. Moreover, as one of the few folks around with any professional experience, I have to admit I also loved being a big fish in a small pond.

Ed Fisher and me playing Bobchinsky and Dobchinsky in *The Inspector General* during the winter of 1947. *Photo by Axel Bahnsen.*

In addition to my monthly USO money, I worked from 7:00 AM to 7:00 PM, and then rehearsed for hours and hours every night. It was a grueling schedule, but I was young, and I was doing what I loved to do most. Exhausted as I'm sure I must have been, I walked around in a state of constant exhilaration. I was doing what I loved best. It was a perfect life.

I kept that schedule for three years, even when the USO money ran out, earning a living doing menial jobs and then working on and appearing in plays at night. Antioch's focus on the classics meant I spent my time concentrating on the works of the masters: Shakespeare, Ben Jonson, O'Neill, Oscar Wilde, Nikolai Gogol, etc.

I was eager to put into practice what I'd learned about the Method from Bromberg and Carnovsky. I worked hard to bring truth and reality onto the stage, to create real human beings other than myself. My approach to acting had totally changed; my

**Me with David Hooks in *Volpone* (1947).
Photo by *Axel Bahnsen.***

**This is me (right) playing Dromio of
Ephesus, with Arthur Oshlag (left) as
Antipholus of Ephesus, in *The Comedy Of
Errors* in 1946. Photo by *Axel Bahnsen.***

interpretation of what I'd learned pushed me more and more in the direction of *becoming* the characters I played.

Each summer, Antioch's Area Theater became a professional stock company with Equity actors recruited from New York and Los Angeles. We were paid Equity stock minimum, plus room and board. In my second season there, I was cast in Emlyn Williams' *Night Must Fall.* I played Danny the Hatbox Murderer, the role I had coveted from the wings in summer stock when I was fifteen. Playing the part of the murderer had always appealed to me. I understood Danny and his deceptive qualities. In addition, feelings of anger left over from my childhood made me a good fit for the part. All these elements helped me develop a convincing interpretation of the role.

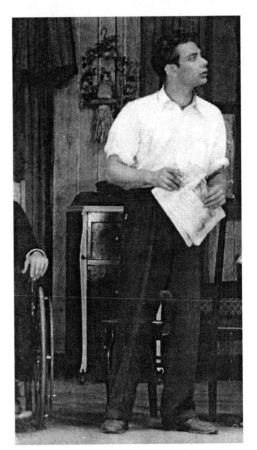

**Me as Danny the Hatbox Murderer in
Night Must Fall (summer 1948). *Photo
by Axel Bahnsen.***

All during rehearsal, I thought of myself as the killer. Both the play and the character possessed me. I would walk down the street muttering to myself about murdering Mrs. Bramson. I was carried away, completely obsessed with the part. I thought that's what Joe and Morris meant by "becoming the character."

Edith Steinberg, a Broadway actress who had retired to Yellow Springs, played the wheelchair-bound victim, Mrs. Bramson. In the last moments of the second act, Danny places a pillow over her head and suffocates her. On opening night, we got to that scene and I—completely consumed by Danny—placed a pillow over Edith's head. I kept it there even after the curtain fell. Two stagehands pulled me off of her just as she began kicking her feet in the air out of pure desperation. Edith caught her breath and stormed out of that wheelchair towards me. "You phony Method actor!" she screamed, slapping me across the face, almost taking my head off.

Thank you, Edith Steinberg. That was a good lesson for me—for any actor, for that matter, with a tendency to be carried away. Never forget, it's only a play. This incident made me rethink the Method as I understood it at that moment. Maybe "becoming the character" wasn't the end-goal after all. I obviously still had much more to learn.

My three years at Antioch and the Area Theater have always stayed with me as the most precious learning experience I've ever had. However, over time, I became increasingly aware that some of the best actors in the summer Equity company had planted themselves there in Ohio and were frightened to return to New York and Los Angeles.

After recognizing that they were never going to leave that safe environment, I became frightened myself that I'd become like them. I'd already had a taste of Broadway and I wanted at least to try to rekindle the acting career I'd left behind in New York. It was time to move on.

Back in New York in 1949, Cliff Hayman came to my rescue once again. He called the famous American playwright Sidney Kingsley on my behalf. Sidney was casting the Chicago company of his critically acclaimed *Detective Story,* and Cliff was convinced the two of us would hit it off. Mr. Kingsley arranged for me to see the New York production of *Detective Story* starring Ralph Bellamy at the Lyceum Theater

Antioch actors Irving Brown and Fran Oliver in *The Merry Wives of Windsor*. Fran Oliver (real name Frances Loud) and I did many plays together during my time at Antioch. Fran was involved in radio and theater in New York from 1936 to 1943. She became the pillar of the Antioch Area Theater in 1947 when her husband joined the faculty at Antioch College. She was a great actress who could have had a career on Broadway but she preferred to stay in Ohio so she could raise her family and continue with community theater.

and to focus on the part of Louis the burglar. The next day I read for Mr. Kingsley and was hired to play Louis in the road company starring Chester Morris.

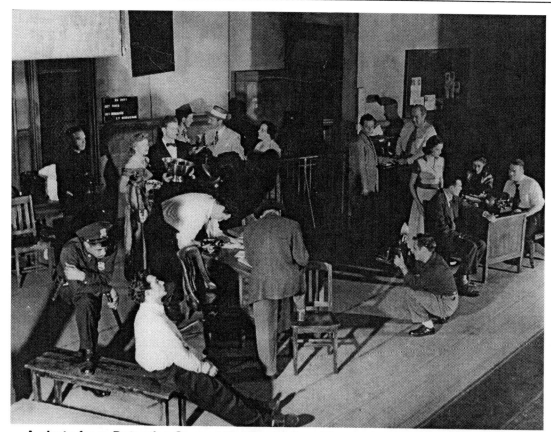

A photo from *Detective Story* at the Blackstone Theater in Chicago in 1949. That's me playing Louis, one of the cat burglars (upper right looking down left). That's the famous Studs Terkel with his back to us. On the extreme right is Chester Morris, a big star in the 1930s. Also pictured are Paul Lipson, Elinor Randel, Walter Starkey, and Marion Winters. *Photo by Fred Fehl.*

During rehearsal, Sidney took me under his wing. "Identify with the character and just do the details," he advised me over and over again.

("Do the details" is a phrase that will come up many times in the pages ahead. It's an element of all good acting. I didn't quite understand it at the time, but something about that phrase stayed with me.)

Sidney's "details" haunted me. What did he mean? When Sidney told an actor to cross downstage, was that a detail? Or when he said, "On the next line, grab her hand." Was that a detail?

Sidney Kingsley (1906–1995) the playwright. *Artwork by Sid Maurer.*

If I'd only felt comfortable asking, "What do you mean?" I could've saved myself tons of work. But not wanting to seem stupid, I never asked what he meant by "details." I know now that the only stupid question is a question unasked. I later found out that details are everything an actor does or says in a scene.

After a few months on the road, *Detective Story* closed at the Blackstone Theater in Chicago in the late spring of 1950. One of the *Detective Story* cast members, Jim Bender, ran a summer stock company in upstate New York, and not long after we wrapped I got a frantic phone call begging me to join his company as a last-minute cast replacement. He wanted me for the important role of Smiley Coy (a nattily dressed, sneaky Hollywood P.R. guy) in Clifford Odets' *The Big Knife.*

I was on the next bus, anxious to get there as fast as I could so I could make the most of what remained of the already short one-week rehearsal period. I wanted to create a fully developed character, but with only four days of rehearsal to do the play, I felt rushed and desperate to find the character.

Alone in my bedroom that first night upstate, worried and unable to sleep, I could at least find some joy in my sexual fantasies. I jumped from fantasy to fantasy until I found the one that did the trick. This time, however, I was struck by the power of those fantasies. Using the same technique, I clearly saw the pivotal scene in my head between Smiley and the lead character, Charlie. Smiley's feelings of dislike for Charlie slowly took me over. Wow! I had made the connection between my sexual fantasy and the author's fantasy.

Just as the details of my sexual fantasy resulted in involuntary automatic behaviors, so did immersing myself in the author's details involuntarily create the behaviors needed in that tough scene. Now I didn't have to act, I could just behave naturally. Once I imagined all the details in my fantasy as I played the scene in my mind, I actually saw my behavior as it went from detail to detail. I felt like Einstein when he discovered "$E = mc^2$." (Well, not quite.)

Through that experience, I discovered one of my primary objectives as an actor: to help tell the author's story through my imagination of the details. By details, I don't mean simply the lines, but the way I say my lines and how I see myself respond to the other actors as I observe the entire scene in my mind (as if I were watching a movie in my head). A deep exploration of the author's fantasy affects everything the actor does, from the tone of his voice to the set of his face and the posture of his body—all those details that are almost involuntary to the actor by the time he's in front of an audience in character.

The rest of that summer and the early fall of 1950, however, were disappointing. It was the sort of period that most actors are forced to endure at some point in their careers. It was a time of destitution, trying to stand alone, facing failure, borrowing money to stay alive, dropping into the pits of being jobless and broke in Manhattan.

Then a miracle happened. Sidney Kingsley somehow found me. He called Ella, who gave him my answering-service number. Robert Whitehead of the Playwrights Company was producing Sidney's adaptation of Arthur Koestler's book *Darkness at Noon*. Sidney, who was also directing, had already cast Kim Hunter, Claude Rains, and Jack Palance, but he couldn't find an actor he liked for the part of Prisoner 202, a political dissident locked away for life in Moscow's notorious Lubyanka Prison.

He gave me the part without an audition, simultaneously saving my ego and my sanity. This time I didn't blow up with hot air, I just went to work trying to develop a compelling character from a two-line part.

Claude Rains (1889–1967) is best known for his great film work, in *Casablanca* and many others. Artwork by Sid Maurer.

In addition to reading Arthur Koestler's original novel, I researched all sorts of articles about the long-term physical and psychological effects of solitary confinement. I learned that many of these prisoners become childlike because they have no name or hope of ever seeing the outside world again. Under the Soviet regime many were imprisoned for simply being devout Russian Orthodox Christians.

Playbill from *Darkness at Noon*.

I found a small antique crucifix that I put in and out of my lips in an obsessive sucking motion. That action with the cross was both religious and childlike. I also spent days at the Central Park Zoo observing the animals pacing up and down in their cages, especially the apes. Most of the cast chuckled at me as I performed these antics during rehearsal. Former Group Theater member Herbert Ratner (who also played a minor part), though, seemed interested in what I was doing, as did Sidney, who actually encouraged me to flesh out the part considerably beyond what he'd written.

My new friend Herb gave me acting tips that were invaluable. "Make things happen," he would say. "Go from moment to moment like building a house. Create a framework." Other than the two lines Sidney had written for the role, everything I did as Prisoner 202 as the lights went up in my cell was unscripted. As Herbert had said, I made it all happen. Often, minor parts need to be embellished in order to complete the author's intentions.

We rehearsed *Darkness at Noon* four weeks in New York, then had a tryout at the Forrest Theater in Philadelphia in December of 1950. We opened on Broadway at the Alvin Theater in January 1951 to good reviews from all the major papers. Claude Rains got raves; they loved Jack Palance and Kim Hunter. And me? Not a single mention. However, the review the entire cast was really waiting to read was Harold Clurman's in that week's issue of the *New Republic*. As a founder of the Group Theater, Clurman was revered in New York theater circles. His review was the only one that mattered to everyone.

Well, he panned the play, but seemed to like the cast: "Most of the actors in *Darkness at Noon* are more than competent. Allan Rich, as Prisoner 202, suggests greater reality than the rest. Claude Rains as Rubashove [*sic*] is always sincere, dignified, and intelligent" (Harold Clurman, *New Republic*, January 1951).

Several cast members resented Clurman's review, and me in particular. Suddenly, the antics in my cell when the lights came up were no longer a laughing matter. Clurman's review clearly validated that old axiom that there are no small parts, only small actors.

Harold Clurman (1901–1980)—theater director, drama critic, and my mentor. *Artwork by Sid Maurer.*

After a respectable half-year's run on Broadway, we closed that June due to Claude Rains's illness. He had just won the Tony Award as the year's best actor but was simply too sick to continue. I felt awful that he was so sick, but I was glad that I'd had a chance to work with him. He was a magnificent actor. Plus I was happy that at last I'd been in a hit play on Broadway!

After *Darkness at Noon* closed, instead of summer stock, I went to summer camp. Good thing, too, because that's where I met my future wife, Elaine. From then on, she became the spine in my life (and what a cook!). By the end of that summer, we were married and going on the road with *Darkness at Noon.* Edward G. Robinson took over the role that Claude Rains had originated on Broadway.

Claude Rains, the Tony winner, was a tough act to follow. He'd played the jailed Russian Commissar with great economy, displaying a quiet power that deeply affected audiences. I waited for the moment every night when he said the line, "As a boy, I loved to study the stars." He conveyed so much with the tone and energy level of that one line that it seemed to sum up the depths of his character's despair. Locked away in his lonely cell, he could only dream about the expansive skies of his youth. That moment moved me to tears almost every night. And I was only listening to him—I couldn't see his face from my cell!

Edward G. Robinson's performance was quite different. While rehearsing the second act of *Darkness at Noon,* Robinson, playing the Russian Commissar, imagined

From left to right: Me, Alan Derric, David Shiner, Daniel Polis, Edward G. Robinson in the national company of *Darkness at Noon.* Photo by Fred Fehl.

his relationship to his secretary, Luba. Staring sullenly through his prison bars, Robinson began to beat his chest and scream, "Luuuuuubaaaaaa, Luuuuuubaaaaaa, Luuuuuubaaaaaa!"

Sidney, who was sitting next to me, leaned over and whispered, "He thinks he's an ape." Fortunately, it was only a rehearsal. Eddie had exploded emotionally, expressing his deep inner feelings for his lost love. When he beat his chest, he took the chance of reaching down to his most primitive self. Great actors take great chances! That's what rehearsals are for.

Eddie Robinson was one of the most respected actors in Hollywood. He played the part with the skill and experience that comes from a generation's worth of important motion picture portrayals and Broadway successes. Robinson was full of feelings and expressed them with the ease of the great actor he was.

Sidney Kingsley had asked me what part I wanted to play in the road company of *Darkness at Noon.* I immediately said Luigi, the forty-five-year-old Italian communist dockworker who's betrayed by Robinson's character, Rubashov. He falsely accuses Luigi of being a fascist, and Luigi answers his charge with a five-minute speech that always brings the house down. I got to play a seven-minute scene with Edward G. Robinson. It was quite a jump from the couple of lines I'd had as Prisoner 202, the

role I had played on Broadway with Claude Rains. What a kick it was for me as a young actor to play every night with one of my idols. First, Claude Rains, now Edward G. Robinson.

After the curtain came down on opening night at Los Angeles' Biltmore Theater, there was a knock on my dressing room door. It was Jack Palance. An extraordinarily voluptuous blond beauty accompanied him. Jack said she'd insisted he bring her backstage. The young lady proceeded to throw her arms around me and plant a big kiss right on my lips.

Marilyn Monroe in 1952. *Photo by Frank Powlony.*

I self-consciously introduced her to Elaine and before I said anything else, she stuck her hand out and said, "I'm Marilyn Monroe and I hope this is your husband because he's a great actor." Her silky smooth voice melted Elaine and me. We were intoxicated. Both of us loved this vulnerable, young, flirtatious, sensitive beauty from then on. I didn't know who the hell she was at the time but I sure was glad Jack had brought her backstage.

During our run of *Darkness at Noon* in Columbus, Ohio, the old crowd from Antioch came to see the show. After the final curtain, they all showed up backstage. Paul Treichler introduced me to Arthur Lithgow (actor John Lithgow's father), the director and producer of Antioch's upcoming summer of Shakespeare's Chronicle Plays. They were going to mount all ten plays that season, everything from *King John* to *Henry VIII.* Lithgow offered me lead roles in *Richard III* and *King John,* as well as the drunken clown Bardolph in *Henry IV,* Parts I and II, and *Henry V,* and Gloucester in *Henry VI,* Part III. Treichler added that it was an Equity company paying the principal actors sixty dollars a week plus room and board. As it was still midwinter and I had at least five months to learn all the lines for those six plays, I readily accepted the challenge.

I opened the season playing the title role in *King John.* At the end of the play, the King takes twenty minutes to die. There were 5,000 people in the outdoor audience. In the middle of my death scene, a large German shepherd

Me as King John with David Hooks. *Photo by Axel Bahnsen*

unexpectedly sauntered onto the stage and sat down next to my deathbed. Believing I was dying, the dog began to squeal and the audience began to titter. I thought

This is the stage for the entire first season of repertory at Antioch for Shakespeare Under the Stars. That #@&*ing German shepherd came up those steps from stage left. *Photo by Axel Bahnsen.*

quickly, grabbed the dog by the muzzle, and played the rest of the scene looking deeply into the dog's sad eyes.

Meanwhile, David Hooks, who played the part of the Bastard, kept whispering in my ear, "Please, look at me." Holding onto the dog for dear life, I didn't even hear him and continued to the end of the scene. After the blackout, I thought the extraordinary ovation I heard was because everyone was touched by the relationship between the dying King and the dog.

Since I had played my death scene to the dog, I anticipated I would receive a very favorable review from the Yellow Springs newspaper. Instead, as I remember, it just gave me a short mention. However, Lithgow got a rave. It went something like this: "Arthur Lithgow's direction was pure magic. Where did he find that dog?"

That's me on the left playing old Uncle Spettigue in *Charley's Aunt*. I was twenty-one and developing my technique. That's David Hooks playing Charlie's Aunt (in drag).
Photo by Axel Bahnsen.

The following day we were to rehearse *Richard II,* but Lithgow, the director, didn't show up. He was found wandering the streets around the theater, desperately searching for the dog, hoping to repeat the "magic" promised by his rave review.

More important than the missing German shepherd, my wife Elaine gave birth prematurely to my son David while I gave birth to the Antioch Shakespeare Festival's *King John.* Elaine never made it to the opening of *King John* and I missed my son's birth. That's show business!

My most challenging moment of the summer came in the fifth act of *Richard III.* Having played Gloucester in *Henry VI,* Part III, the previous night, I played Richard III in a matinee at about 3:30 PM on a very sunny day. My line was, "It is now dead midnight. Cold fearful drops stand my trembling flesh." My imagination of that moment, as I really felt it was midnight in my mind, was so strong that no sound came from the audience. Somehow, I had convinced them I was in complete darkness.

It was a great summer, and since I wasn't in *Henry VIII,* the last play of the season, Elaine, the baby, and I returned to the Big Apple. We settled into an apartment on

West 75th Street for a week or so. I then called my agent, Lucille Phillips, who began sending me out for guest roles on various live TV shows.

Over the next three months, I played various small parts in live televisions shows like *Playhouse 90, Studio One, Kraft Television Theatre,* and *You Are There,* before landing a lead in an episode of NBC's *Philco Playhouse.* What a break! Once again, I was riding high. I was to receive a good salary for the two week's work. Rehearsals were supposed to begin that Monday morning.

When I arrived at the NBC rehearsal hall, though, the casting director, Bill Nichols, greeted me. "NBC is very sorry, but they've decided to go another way," he informed me. "However, Allan, please remember that NBC loves your work. We will, of course, use you sometime in the future." He sweet-talked me while I was in a stunned and vulnerable state.

When I returned home, I called Lucille. She asked me if I'd signed my contract. I said, 'Not yet.' "

"Well," she said, "in that case, they were within their rights to let you go."

I didn't play another role on network television for the next eight years. From that moment in 1952—until 1961—every casting agent and talent agent working in TV turned me down.

Late in December of 1952, Harold Clurman threw me a lifeline by casting me in the George

Me in *Darkness at Noon* as Prisoner 202 at the Alvin Theater in 1951.

Tabori play *The Emperor's Clothes.* I figured Clurman must have remembered his review of me in *Darkness at Noon* the previous year.

During the rehearsal period of *The Emperor's Clothes,* I was fortunate to have extensive conversations with Harold Clurman. He was a real master of the theater, and his words have stayed with me all these years: "It's all in the play," he would tell me again and again. "Just keep reading the play."

Harold was the co-founder of the Group Theater. He had directed more than twenty Broadway plays, including *Awake and Sing, Men in White, Paradise Lost, Golden Boy, Rocket to the Moon,* and *Night Music.* From 1937 to 1942, he was the Group Theater's sole director. His books and essays are important contributions to 20th-century dramatic criticism. His *The Fervent Years* and *On Directing* have become bibles to the New York theater community. As rigorous as he may sometimes have been, I'll always love who he was—a daring, insightful, brilliant man. And a mensch, too.

Harold took a big chance and cast the blind British character actor Esmond Knight in one of the lead roles in *The Emperor's Clothes.* Though he'd basically gone blind by this point, Esmond was sure that with rehearsal he'd have no problem carrying off whatever blocking Harold worked out for him. Esmond didn't want the public to know he'd completely lost his sight, and Harold felt confident he could pull it off. I remember one day during rehearsal, Harold gave Esmond a simple piece of emotionally motivated direction Esmond apparently didn't like. He quietly turned to Harold and in his clipped West End accent said, "My dear, Mr. Clurman, I've been in the theater for forty years. I just say the words, collect my salary, and piss off home."

Harold laughed good-naturedly and said, "Of course, Esmond, I understand perfectly." This was a perfect example of Harold's humanity. Meanwhile, he always found some clever way to get Esmond to do exactly what he wanted. Actually, Harold always found a way to get what he wanted from all of us. The play ran for three weeks and closed late in February of 1953.

I spent the next several months working a series of odd jobs trying to keep my family afloat. It wasn't long before I was completely out of money. I grew increasingly angry and despondent. I'd done a good job with all my other TV work. Why had I been fired from my first lead before I'd even had a chance to show them what I could do? Why had my TV career suddenly gone cold?

Fortunately, my father-in-law, Irving, supplied us with a housekeeper to care for little David while Elaine and I looked for work. We both found jobs selling subscriptions to the *New York Times* on the telephone. Elaine's mother, Frieda, took care of little David while we worked every night until 10 PM.

My low point was working for a company named Santa Calling. I spent all fall in a Santa Claus costume going door to door selling toys. Unfortunately, the two girls who ran the company ran off with all the money before we could deliver the toys. Consequently, all the Santa Clauses were arrested by the police. Lucky for me, my cousin, Eddie Frankle, the family's lawyer, got me (and the other Santas) off. The police went after the girls, but I'm not sure they were ever caught. What a racket!

I didn't realize for a full year that I was in the thick of the Red Scare and McCarthyism. One fateful day, at the famous Astor Drugstore (the actors' hangout on 45th and Broadway), I was informed that I was listed in *Red Channels,* an infamous magazine published by an ex–FBI agent and a right-wing TV producer who were determined to ruin any actor, director, or writer who was left-leaning.

I had been on the Theater Action Committee to Free Willie Magee (a black man who had been falsely accused of rape), and the men behind *Red Channels* saw the Committee as a subversive organization. In their eyes, the Theater Action Committee was nothing but a communist front, and they routinely attempted to silence its organizers. At least I'd been blacklisted standing up for what I believe in: civil rights, freedom of speech, the Bill of Rights, and everything America is supposed to represent.

Among those listed in *Red Channels* were Stella Adler, Leonard Bernstein, Aaron Copland, Dashiel Hammett, Lillian Hellman, Burl Ives, Arthur Miller, Dorothy Parker, and Pete Seeger, to name a few. Though I surely didn't feel much comfort back then, I now feel privileged to have been included in such esteemed company.

Red Channels magazine went to all the ad agencies and TV networks, and if your name appeared in it, you were not to be hired. I was actually relieved to hear that I'd been listed. I'd been frightened that I wasn't working because I'd lost my talent.

In early 1954, Cliff Hayman produced a road production of *The Postman Always Rings Twice*. He hired me as the assistant stage manager and offered me the role of the priest in the second act. The production featured two notorious actors: Barbara Payton (a Jean Harlow type) and Tom Neal (star of the film noir classic *Detour;* he'd beaten up Franchot Tone in a much-publicized Hollywood fistfight over Payton's affections in '51). After they both performed drunk early in the Chicago run, it was such a scandal that the play closed and the tickets for the rest of the two-week engagement had to be refunded. (Barbara later turned to prostitution; Tom shot his wife in 1965 and did seven years in prison.)

By 1955, the realities of family life forced me away from acting to, of all places, Wall Street. Suddenly I was living and meeting all of the characters I was destined to play—crooks, hustlers, lawyers, judges, CEOs, accountants—people fighting and scratching to make a buck. I was wheeling and dealing in stocks, using my creative imagination to relate to this new world of commerce and capitalism.

I concluded that it is all acting. If I made a good sale in the bond market, I would joke with Elaine that I was a feature player that week. After making a huge commission, I would tell Elaine I was a star that week as I handed

That's me as Richard III with Edythe Hartt as Margaret during my days at Antioch. *Photo by Axel Bahnsen.*

her the check. I may not have been strictly acting, but let's just say I made good money while constantly honing my craft. In our spare time, we started to collect art we liked—mostly Modern paintings and drawings.

I didn't know it at the time, but this life experience was yet another piece of the puzzle. No matter how I made a living, I knew in my heart that eventually—when Elaine and I had saved enough money—I would somehow begin my acting career again.

In the spring of 1956, Joe Papp (head of "Shakespeare in the Park" in New York City) was holding auditions for *Richard III.* When I found out about it, I left my brokerage office and auditioned for the role. It was an open call, and I truly believed I had a good shot, since I had played Richard III in 1952. I thought I *was* Richard. I gave a great reading but came in second to George C. Scott. Papp offered me the part of Ratcliff, but I foolishly turned it down and went back to my office on Wall Street. Mistake, mistake.

Never turn down a part when you're on your way up. This is particularly true if the part gives you an opportunity to work with other gifted, vital artists. Too bad I didn't remember the axiom that had served me well as Prisoner 202: "There are no small parts, there are only small actors."

I would advise everyone starting out today to take any part they can get—except pornography or unreasonable nudity—on the way up. For me, though, it was different. Had I won the part of

Me with my wife Elaine, son David, and daughter Marion circa 1960.

Richard, I would have gambled. However, since George C. Scott had won the role instead, I decided not to take a chance with my family's financial well-being. I went back to Wall Street, happy for the moment that I was making a good living for my family.

Many years later, Joe Papp hung up on me when I phoned him to let him know I was interested in playing the title role in his upcoming Shakespeare in the Park production of *Richard II*. He got even with me. When you reject them, they never forget.

Renee Taylor (center) and I were in Harold Clurman's after-theater class together. Years later, Donna Dixon (left) was one of my students and we eventually worked together on a TV pilot.

Toward the end of 1956, I was accepted into Harold Clurman's after-theater class. These classes were for working actors, as well as Harold's favorites who were momentarily out of work (like me). Of course, I was the only stockbroker there.

Harold's class was perhaps the apex of acting classes. His criticisms and stories have stayed with everyone who ever studied or worked with him, and they've become an integral part of our creative lives.

Harold's criticism was simply an up-or-down vote; either he believed your performance or he didn't. If he didn't believe you, he asked that you read the play again and do the scene again and again until you got it right. If you asked him what you had done wrong, he'd tell you to take a private lesson with an acting coach. "I'm not a teacher, I'm a director," he'd admonish. "You're supposed to be a professional Broadway actor, so act like one. Keep in mind your name is not Bernhardt or Duse."

Even though his criticisms were stinging, the twinkle in his eyes would make you laugh, especially if you were the actor he was addressing. You somehow believed he wanted you to be the best actor you possibly could be. That was his way of getting through to you.

He once told the class about how he had been called by a Hollywood mogul to replace director John Huston on a film. Harold had told him that he didn't know much about film directing, whereas John Huston knew a great deal. The offer of thousands of dollars and three months in Hollywood wasn't for him. He had turned the mogul down. He told our class that Hollywood wasn't real to him—his favorite New York restaurants were real. His students, books, and close friends were the things that were real to him. That was Harold: a man so dedicated to his work and his students that he couldn't conceive of selling out (as he saw it), no matter how great the opportunity might appear to be. His attitude, deportment, knowledge, personality, passion, and humor were an inspiration to all of us who were part of his life.

In 1961, Herbert Ratner got me a new agent, Georgia Gilley, and I began to go out on TV auditions again. It'd been eight years since my last job in television, but I landed four parts in a row: I played a witness opposite E. G. Marshall in *The Defenders,* a cab driver in *Naked City,* a lawyer with George C. Scott in *East Side, West Side,* and a supporting role in an episode of *The Armstrong Circle Theater* starring Charles Durning.

The following year, though, Georgia was lured to Hollywood. Without an agent making calls on my behalf, I went right back to work selling stocks as an officer of Carroll Company, my brokerage firm in

The great surrealist master, Salvador Dalí, posed for a picture in front of my art gallery on Madison Avenue.

Manhattan. I had taken time off from the firm to do the four gigs, so there was no time to find a new agent. I had to go back to work in the stock market. That was a sure way to earn good money.

The fact was that I didn't want to go looking for an agent. I preferred going back to work as a broker. I loved wheeling and dealing on Wall Street. There was no way that I was going to put my family in jeopardy looking for work as an actor.

The summer of 1961 was the best twelve weeks I ever had in the stock market. There were days I earned two to three thousand dollars. The kids went to camp and Elaine and I seriously began to collect art. The good times, however, soon ended.

In May of 1962, the stock market took a sharp dive. It went down over 5 percent in one day. My firm lost its shirt and so did I. Luckily, I was offered a job in an art gallery owned by a former boss. He knew I could sell stock and he also knew I'd become a passionate art collector. Within one month, I had doubled the gallery's sales. Soon after, one of my clients offered me a partnership in a new gallery on 50th Street at Third Avenue. By 1965, I owned that gallery on my own.

In 1966, Wynn Handman of New York's American Place Theater called me to do *Journey of the Fifth Horse,* a new play set in nineteenth-century Russia. It was by Ronald Ribman, a young, gifted playwright. Apparently, Wynn

This portrait of me hung center stage in *Journey of the Fifth Horse.*

remembered my performance as Chernov in *Anastasia* at the Hyde Park Playhouse in the summer of 1958; he wanted someone who'd play a Russian with a convincing accent.

At the first reading of *Journey of the Fifth Horse,* I met a young actor, Dustin Hoffman. He was a twenty-eight year-old kid and he did all the details—very quietly. It was only our first read-through, but Dustin allowed the material to transport him and change him so completely that the whole cast was moved by his cold reading as it transformed into a full-blown performance. I was amazed by his acting ability. He got even better during rehearsal and ultimately won the Obie Award for Best Actor (Off-Broadway) in 1966 for his performance in *Journey of the Fifth Horse.*

From 1966 to 1972, I focused on the Allan Rich Gallery at 787 Madison Avenue. I ran a side business

This is me posing in front of George Hurrell's photograph of Marlene Dietrich. I became his publisher in 1979.

I played the role of District Attorney Herman Tauber in *Serpico. Photo courtesy of Paramount Pictures. SERPICO © Paramount Pictures. All Rights Reserved.*

publishing graphics by many 20th-century masters, such as Picasso, Dalí, Agam, and Miro. I also sold paintings, watercolors, and drawings of some of the great School of Paris giants: Picasso, Chagall, Utrillo, Vlaminck, etc. In addition, I ran charity auctions at churches and synagogues in all five boroughs of New York City.

By 1972, after I'd made a bunch of "fuck you" money in the art business, I finally felt that my family was in excellent financial condition, and I could safely say, now it's my turn. I decided to call an actor's manager who happened to live in my building on West 71st in Manhattan. That fine lady's name was Betty Geffen.

Betty Geffen looked over my old résumé, with all my Broadway credits and road tours, and decided to help me. She began to send me out. I auditioned for commercials, episodic TV, theater, movies, and, lo and behold, I landed the part of the District Attorney in Sidney Lumet's *Serpico.*

Serpico was my springboard to thirty years of work in movies and television. The role of D.A. Tauber was based on Burton Roberts, who, at the time of the actual events, was head of the commission investigating widespread New York City Police Department corruption. Frank Serpico, who was an undercover detective, had blown the whistle on squad after squad of cops who were (to one degree or another) either involved with or turning a blind eye to drug trafficking. He'd been ostracized because he wouldn't take any drug money. D.A. Tauber implies that he plans to take the case to the very top—indicting even the Department higher-ups who had turned a blind eye to Serpico's earlier complaints—but in the end Tauber disappoints. He wants to help Serpico, but he will go only so far. In the end, the film implies that he's a political animal who simply can't afford to name names.

By the time *Serpico* was in production, the real D.A., Burton Roberts, had become a circuit court judge. I met with him, and the man radiated dignity, warmth, power, and integrity. It was a huge help for my research. Now it behooved me to find a way to express all those traits in my opening scene.

As I make my first entrance in the film, I've traveled a great distance to see Serpico, and the first thing I see when I get there is him trying to beat a hasty exit from the building. I literally have to block his way to grab a moment of his time. I compliment him and tell him I'll take his case all the way to the grand jury. While saying my line, a great detail came to me. After the first take, I said to director Lumet, "I'd like to take my hat and coat off and hand it to an extra who looks like a law clerk. I think that detail will make my character look more powerful."

Before this scene with Al Pacino in *Serpico,* I suggested to the director, Sidney Lumet, that I needed someone to take my hat and coat while I'm talking to Serpico. Lumet asked why, to which I answered, "It will give my character more power." Lumet shouted, "Get this man an extra." *Photo courtesy of Paramount Pictures. SERPICO © Paramount Pictures. All Rights Reserved.*

Lumet smiled and turned to the first assistant director, "Get this man an extra that looks like a law clerk." With that additional detail, the moment clicked for me. It made my character seem important and added tension to my interaction with Al Pacino.

Sidney Lumet really loves his actors. He was wide open to all of our suggestions. He loved it when the cast would improvise details that weren't in the script but helped tell the story more effectively. Every time he printed a take, he'd give the actors a big hug. He always made me feel ten feet tall. Everyone always feels relaxed and secure on Lumet's sets; it's one of the smartest ways to encourage everyone to do their best work.

During the airing of the 1973 Academy Awards, a clip from *Serpico* was shown. It was my last scene with Pacino. He's come to my office to confront me. The contrast between my mellow delivery (earnestly promising Serpico a detective's gold shield for his bravery in the line of duty) and Pacino's angry response (because I had blocked him from naming names to the grand jury) made for a scene full of emotional sparks. Millions of people saw that broadcast.

My friend and Oscar-winning actor, Red Buttons.

Betty suggested that I take ads out in the trades thanking the production company and the Academy for using that scene. I received only one response from Hollywood. John Crosby, an agent at International Creative Management (ICM), called my manager and said, "If your client ever gets to LA, tell him to look me up."

I wasted no time checking John Crosby out, and I was encouraged by what I heard. As fate would have it, Elaine and I were going to Las Vegas for a brief vacation, so with a simple change of destinations we headed to Los Angeles instead. I immediately looked up John Crosby.

When I met him at his ICM office, I told Crosby, "I can play anything John Barrymore, Edward G. Robinson, Claude Rains, or James Cagney could play. Can you get me a job?"

He stared at me for a moment, picked up the phone, and said, "Get me Joe D'Agosta at Universal." While waiting for the call to go through, he explained that

Joe D'Agosta was the casting director for the TV show *Baretta*. After a pause, he continued. "Hello, Joe. I'm sitting here with an actor who says he can play anything John Barrymore, Edward G. Robinson, Claude Rains, or James Cagney could have played. You've seen his work. He played the D.A. in *Serpico*. He was the guy opposite Pacino in the scene they just used at the Oscars." Another pause, then: "Good, I'm glad you remember. I'll send him right over."

Me with Fran Drescher, my friend and a truly great comedienne. *Photo courtesy of Orly Halevy and Diana Ezra Photography.*

Crosby gave me the address and directions to Universal Studios. Joe D'Agosta and I immediately hit it off, and he got me a reading with the director of *Baretta*. By the time I returned to my hotel, there was a message from Crosby that the script was being sent by messenger and I would start work the following Monday.

In 1976 Elaine and I closed out our life in Manhattan and moved ourselves to Los Angeles, where we've lived ever since. John Crosby remained my agent for seven years until he went to ABC as Vice President of Casting in 1982.

In the three decades since

My longtime friend Dan Aykroyd with me at my home in the Hollywood Hills.] The list goes on and on. It's been a long and wonderful journey. As a matter of fact, I wrapped my latest job, a coming-of-age movie called *My Sexiest Year* in May of 2006. It was my sixty-eighth film role (and still counting).

Serpico, I've worked consistently on stage, in television, and in films. I consider myself a lucky, grateful old actor to have worked with some of the finest directors in

Me with Michael Douglas at my friend Zack Norman's home in the Hollywood Hills.

Hollywood: Alan Alda, Graham Clifford, Martha Coolidge, Francis Ford Coppola, Barry Levinson, Ron Maxwell, Robert Redford, Steven Spielberg, and Irwin Winkler.

Moreover, as a character actor, I've gotten to work opposite all sorts of stars— Dan Aykroyd, Lucille Ball, Nell Carter, Robert DeNiro, Donna Dixon, Michael Douglas, Fran Drescher, Ralph Fiennes, Morgan Freeman, Jessica Lange, Demi Moore, Al Pacino, Renee Taylor.

In addition to being my agent and giving me that extra push, John Crosby was also responsible for me becoming an acting coach. Over dinner one night, he voiced

Me with John Crosby at my 50th wedding anniversary party. *Photo by Chris Jurgenson.*

some concerns about a new client, a gorgeous, talented model who was perfect for a role in a major film opposite a bankable name. He told me that though she had no prior acting experience, she was such a sensitive and intelligent lady he was confident that with a little help she could be a major star.

I knew John had an amazing eye for talent, so I suggested taking a crack at coaching her for her big audition. I relished the chance to coach a beautiful, intelligent, sensitive young woman. What could be better? By the way,

John, no charge. Meanwhile, she came in number two for the role, but everyone at the studio was suddenly excited about her. Soon she landed the first of many major films, and from that point on, my career as a coach was off and running.

Because of the coaching opportunities sent my way via John Crosby, I had to learn to verbalize and encapsulate my way of working. Over time I began to develop and teach a simple acting technique that my students have found quite useful. Those early coaching experiences are the inspiration for *A Leap from the Method.*

I developed a series of questions that help me greatly while approaching any role, and I've used this same basic approach to every part, both as an actor and as a coach. Did I tell the story? Did I experience the back-story? Did I do the details? Was I economical? Was the situation important enough to me?

Observing my students over time, I found I learned at least as much from them as they learned from me. When struggling to communicate to an actor

Konstantin Stanislavsky (1863–1938), creator of "the Method." *Artwork by Sid Maurer.*

who wasn't following what I meant, I would discover much more about what I was trying to explain in the first place!

I also began to take a closer look at what has been written about Stanislavsky's Method and its effects on acting through the 20th century. Much of what he taught is still useful, but much of it is open to interpretation, or dead-ends in places that are helpful only as examples of what NOT to do. Still, Stanislavsky is to acting what Freud is to modern psychology. Without him, there would be nothing to leap from. As frustrating or hazy as some of his work may appear, the profound effect it had on acting has forever changed our profession.

CHAPTER 2
THE METHOD AND THE GROUP THEATER

Like most actors who began their careers after the 1930s, I learned from teachers who were deeply influenced by the Method. Love it or hate it, Stanislavsky's emotional and psychological approach to acting (popularized in America by the Group Theater as "the Method") has exhilarated, confounded, inspired, and changed the face of theater as we know it.

When Stanislavsky began his career in the latter part of the nineteenth century, many actors here and in Europe used a stiff, declamatory technique of acting. Instead of trying to display real feelings, for the most part their performances were completely external.

Notable exceptions to this approach were the famous character actors of the period who inspired Stanislavsky: Eleonora Duse and Tommaso Salvini in Italy, Sarah Bernhardt and Talma in France. Stanislavsky wondered how they were able to connect so

Sarah Bernhardt (1844–1923) was perhaps the most famous actress of the 19th century. _Artwork by Sid Maurer._

effortlessly with their audiences. Was there something repeatable in the way they worked that allowed them to achieve their amazing results?

Like these talents, the great American actress Laurette Taylor broke with tradition and brought a semblance of psychological realism to all of her roles. At the end of her career she starred in Tennessee Williams' *The Glass Menagerie* (1945). Both critics and audiences were overwhelmed by the simple power of her performance.

When Laurette Taylor was asked what she thought was the most important thing about acting, she said: "Personality is more important than beauty, but imagination is more important than both. Acting is the physical representation of a mental picture and the projection of an emotional concept." Whether she'd encountered Stanislavsky or not, they were clearly kindred spirits in their approaches.

Italian actor Tommaso Salvini (1829–1915) was considered the greatest actor of his time. *Artwork by Sid Maurer.*

For most of his adult life, Stanislavsky searched and worked to find a system for creating truth and inspiration on the stage. He wanted audiences to look at performances as approximations of reality. Ideally, spectators would be so drawn into the drama that they would forget the world around them and experience the inner feelings of the characters right along with the actors.

He began to develop ways to demonstrate and explain to his students what he had learned from examining Duse, Salvini, and the others. George Bernard Shaw had famously observed that audiences were stunned when Duse's face literally turned crimson upon receipt of a former lover's flowers in the play *Magda*.

Stanislavsky realized that they each strove to go beyond what was on the written page; they sought to deepen and extend the details supplied by the author to achieve new levels of inspiration. Unfortunately, those great moments that inspired

Stanislavsky are forever lost to us. Theater is fleeting; its moments of greatness are gone as soon as they occur. They live on only in memory and the small glimpses recorded in the writings of the critics and historians of a given period.

Fortunately, though, we have a growing body of film performances which exemplify the sort of naturalistic realism Stanislavsky talked (and tried to write) about. Robert Duvall's performance in *To Kill a Mockingbird* is a perfect example of an actor going beyond the material. His body language, his eyes and almost deadpan expressions spoke loudly to me as he portrayed a deaf-mute. From the first moment he appeared on the screen I was sure he was not an actor but a real deaf-mute the director had found in town. He frightened me just as he scared

Some of the best performances ever captured on film were by my friend Jennifer Jason Leigh in movies like *Last Exit to Brooklyn*, *Single White Female*, and *Washington Square*.

the little girl as she passed his run-down house. In the final moments, he murders the villain off screen and saves the children, unexpectedly exposing a gentle, quiet, loving personality, totally understood by the little girl. His wordless—but emotionally towering performance—perfectly conveys his transition from scary outsider (whom we, like the children, fear) to someone we trust so completely that we know the little girl could hardly be in safer hands when they walk off together at the film's conclusion.

Trying to find a system or a way of working that would satisfy his dreams of actors going beyond the written material led Stanislavsky to amazing success with his students, as well as influence on the great directors and actors he worked with in the internationally famous Moscow Art Theater.

Back in the mid-1920s, Stanislavsky brought his groundbreaking ensemble to America. They performed Chekhov, Gogol, Gorky, and others on Broadway and received wonderful reviews. Cheryl Crawford, Lee Strasberg, and Harold Clurman

Lee Strasberg (1901–1982) co-founder of the Group Theater. *Artwork by Sid Maurer.*

were thoroughly inspired by what they saw on the stage. They came away wishing to create a similar troupe in America.

In 1931—in the middle of the Great Depression—Clurman, Crawford, and Strasberg formed the Group Theater and changed the face of American theater as we knew it. Everyone in their ensemble worked collectively to create a reality on the stage using an approach patterned after the acclaimed work done by Stanislavsky and the Moscow Art Theater.

The Group produced *Men in White,* written by Sidney Kingsley. It was a huge success and led to a series of powerful and relevant productions. In every subsequent work, the cast and crew strove for a naturalistic style that reflected the harsh realities people faced just outside the theater doors. Strikingly of-the-moment at the time, many of these plays have become often-produced modern classics: *Awake and Sing*, *Golden Boy*, *Rocket to the Moon*, *Waiting for Lefty.*

Despite Stanislavsky's monumental influence on theater in America—indeed, around the world—capturing his system in writing proved to be impossible. Despite three books (*An Actor Prepares, Building a Character,* and *Creating a Role*), plus many essays and papers, he still considered his work incomplete at best. As he wrote to Maxim Gorky in a February 1933 letter excerpted here:

My life has been a fortunate one. It shaped itself. I was just a tool in its hands. Yet this good fortune lays on me the obligation to hand on to others, before I die, what life has given to me. Yet how difficult it is to share one's experience in such a complex process as the creative work of an actor. When one is in personal touch with students one can show, demonstrate, act out things which are difficult to formulate in written words. To act out—that is our sphere. But when one takes pen in hand all the words needed to define feelings run away and hide themselves. I have harnessed my mind to the task of putting on paper, as concisely and clearly as I can, what a beginning actor should know. Such a book is needed if only to put an end to all the twisted interpretations put on my so-called "system" which, in the way it is presently being taught, can put young actors on quite the wrong path.

(From a letter to Maxim Gorky, dated 2/10/33. Excerpted from *Stanislavsky's Legacy,* first published in 1958.)_

This letter saddens me; I empathize with Stanislavsky's inability to put down on paper what he was able so freely to communicate to his students in person. I wish I knew what he meant by "the wrong path" and which elements of his books and essays were misinterpreted. It must have pained him deeply when he was unable to find the right words to lead acting students—including his own—toward a readable, repeatable system for portraying real emotions on the stage.

Then I consider how I found myself on "the wrong path" when I almost murdered Edith Steinberg during a performance. Having read Stanislavsky's letter to Gorky while preparing this book, I now comprehend how confounded I was by the countless concepts floating around concerning the Method. It's no wonder that the years following Stanislavsky's death have given rise to confusing, misguided, and overly complex interpretations of his "system." In evaluating many of the famous acting teachers since Stanislavsky, I've come across approaches that he would barely recognize, let alone endorse.

Consider exercises like "private moments," where an actor performs something private in front of the class as a way to overcome inhibition. Picking one's nose in public is at best unnecessary, and probably a rapid acceleration down the wrong path. From my way of working, it has nothing to do with acting and seems to be psychotherapy inappropriately delivered by an acting teacher instead of a psychotherapist.

Then there's the "repetition" exercise, where an actor and his partner speak the same word or phrase to each other repeatedly as a way to practice reacting. Though reacting to one's fellow actors is an important part of acting, without the context of story and circumstance, it seems like a waste of time.

Finally, there are "emotional or affective memory" exercises. In order to display real feelings on the stage, the actor recalls specific memories from his own life—moments of anger or sadness—and then relives them as dictated by the script and story. Though Lee Strasberg was an ardent supporter of an approach using "emotional memory" almost from the start, several members of the Group eventually took particular exception to its use. They felt it disconnected them from their ability to create a believable reality in the moment.

On a 1934 trip to Paris, Group member Stella Adler (the daughter of two of New York's best-known Yiddish theater stars) met and studied with Stanislavsky. He was in the City of Lights being treated for emphysema. While there, he taught several acting classes—most notably to students studying opera—and Stella studied with him for a few weeks. She asked Stanislavsky about "emotional memory." He was surprised anyone was still using that technique; he told her he'd abandoned it as unworkable many years before. When she got back to the Group Theater, Adler informed everyone of Stanislavsky's current position on emotional memory. Strasberg, though, continued to use it; he believed it was a useful tool.

Adler—who later went on to a career as one of America's most revered acting teachers—totally disagreed with Strasberg's approach. In a televised interview in the early 1980s, she explained why she didn't like having to substitute an emotional memory from her real life for what the author had set forth for the

Stella Adler (1901–1992) learned directly from Stanislavsky. *Artwork by Sid Maurer.*

character: "I didn't like that whole concept," Adler remembered. "I wanted to be in the dramatic sense of the author and the author's characters, and I fought Strasberg on it." Stella wanted to use the author's back-story (or create one herself that stayed within the author's intentions) instead of creating a substitute happening from her own life that had nothing to do with the play. She preferred to allow the circumstances supplied by the author—the events that take place within the world of the drama itself—to stimulate her imagination moment to moment, resulting in the feelings or emotions required to push the story forward. She didn't want to separate herself from the story and think of a memory outside of the play. In spite of her opposition to emotional memory, she decided to remain with the group while it slowly began to deteriorate.

As Wendy Smith detailed in *Real Life Drama,* her excellent history of the Group Theater and its eventual dissolution, by 1937, after a half-dozen years of entertainment and enlightenment, things at the Theater were really going sour. Many members of the Group collectively wrote a scathing letter of complaint to its founders. There were many contributing factors to their unhappiness. First, there was the dissatisfaction with Lee Strasberg's direction of the play they were currently preparing, *Johnny Johnson.* In addition, they were dissatisfied with Harold Clurman's management of the Theater's business dealings. Moreover, they mentioned Cheryl Crawford's frustration at not being used creatively, which severely limited her contributions to the Group.

In the wake of that letter, Strasberg and Crawford quit the Group. Clurman stayed on for another four years, during which he directed an acclaimed revival of Clifford Odets' *Awake and Sing*, as well as several other well-received productions. The Group formally disbanded in 1941.

Many of the Group Theater's actors, directors, and writers forged successful careers in Hollywood. Even before the Group Theater's decline, several of the members had left for Hollywood and the promise of a better living. Franchot Tone, Frances Farmer, and John Garfield became major stars. (Special thanks to Grove Atlantic for allowing me to paraphrase pages 288 through 298 of Wendy Smith's book.)

Elia Kazan became a renowned movie director, but later, during the days of the communist witch-hunt in Hollywood, he made the choice to name names. Many of those Kazan exposed were former Group members, who never forgave him. By naming names, he retained his power and influence in Hollywood rather than being blacklisted like his old friends.

Me with Robert DeNiro and director Irwin Winkler on the set of *Guilty By Suspicion*.

In 1947, Kazan and Bobby Lewis created the Actors Studio as a place for actors to work and develop their craft. In 1949, Lee Strasberg joined the Studio and immediately took charge of teaching duties. This is where he continued his adaptation of Stanislavsky's system, which included "private moments" and "emotional memory" exercises. In spite of these two controversial concepts, his way of working influenced hundreds of young actors, many of whom became film stars: James Dean, Al Pacino, and Robert DeNiro, among them. Those stars have in turn had a profound impact on hundreds of actors, teachers, and university professors all over the world. Therefore, Stanislavsky—misunderstood or not—has become the irrefutable and foremost influence on the way actors approach their craft and the way that craft is taught.

There are many different interpretations of the Stanislavsky Method floating around. Therefore, the actor has a dilemma. He's constantly trying to accept what he believes works and discard what he believes doesn't work, but he's never quite sure which is which. My own experience as an acting coach has repeatedly demonstrated that people who have never studied at all rapidly digest what I mean with less confusion than those who have studied with several other Method teachers.

So, where do I sit in the wake of all those interpretations? I sit on the back of Stanislavsky's idea that acting is organic and comes from the imagination of the actor. While there may be many myths and misconceptions complicating matters, whether as an acting coach or as a performer, I always strive for a simple, direct approach. That's my true leap from the Method, at least as it's become popularized today.

CHAPTER 3
THE THREE MYTHS OF ACTING

When I begin to teach a class or coach an actor, the first thing I do is dispose of what I call the three myths of acting. Acting teachers, particularly Method acting coaches, put an inordinate amount of emphasis on the concept of truth and the use of the word "character," but the most frustrating thing is their misuse of the word "talent." The worst mistake acting teachers make is judging actors, having them come in and audition, and then deciding from those auditions who has talent and who doesn't, who they'll accept into an acting class and who they won't. In my opinion, this is a terrible disservice to up-and-coming actors. I'll teach anyone who's passionate about wanting to learn.

THE FIRST MYTH: TALENT

The first myth concerns the use of the word "talent." Entertainment professionals talk about talent as though it's the rarest and most precious commodity. People keep saying, "he's talented," "she's untalented," "he has no talent," "she's a big talent," "he's a small talent." That's actually a lot of crap. The truth is we all have talent. Talent means potential. Every one of us has enormous potential. That's what we human beings are—potential. All shapes and all sizes.

Unfortunately, much of what's innate in us is stifled in the first few years of our lives. Few of us learn how to rear children. It's not taught in schools and many families have long histories of doing it badly.

My grandkids, Julia, Miles, and little Ruby.

Fortunately, some people have the good luck to be raised by parents who encourage their children's natural creativity. Still others find teachers who nurture their desire to learn, or meet people along the way who inspire them to achieve their potential. We all need catalysts, people to push us forward. Harold Clurman in particular was there to give me a well-deserved shove when I needed one. I felt stranded during my first three months in Hollywood. The phone didn't ring and I was deeply in the depths of doubting my "talent." In the throes of desperation, I picked up the phone and called Harold. After several rings an impatient voice said, "Yes?"

"Harold, it's Allan Rich."

"What is it, Allan?"

I paused for a moment and then asked, "Do I have any talent?"

Harold snapped back, "Read your fucking notice," and hung up. I knew he was referring to the positive review he wrote of me for *Darkness at Noon*. He made me feel silly and embarrassed. I thought deeply about what Harold said. That was an important hang up for any actor with an important "hang-up." I concluded at that moment that we are all "talented." I never asked that question again and passed that insight, from then on, to all my subsequent students. That knowledge led to my conclusion that we humans have little or no instinct.

Human beings are born with less innate knowledge than most other animals. A tiny spider can instinctively build a web of tremendous size and complexity. It would take forever to learn how a spider weaves its web. However, we human beings have something enormously special in our heads—the most sophisticated computer known to man. We can program our own computers more completely and with greater complexity than any other creature. With our capacity for questioning, learning, and growth, we can be anything we want to be; our potential can be developed and released if we desire it deeply enough.

If you really insist on considering yourself talented, and you come to an acting problem that you can't solve, watch out, because when your idealized image of believing you are talented collides with the despised image of discovering that maybe you're not as talented as you think, the result can be devastating. It's better to give up the word "talent" and go to work.

Talent is merely desire combined with the drive and ability to work hard. Desire is the key. Desire combined with hard work can fulfill your potential.

> "There can be no art without virtuosity, without practice, without technique, and the greater the talent, the more they are needed."
> **Konstantin Stanislavsky** (1863–1938) from *Collected Works*, Vol. 1, *My Life in Art, Stanislavsky's Legacy*

THE SECOND MYTH: TRUTH

"You must tell the truth" is repeated time and again by acting teachers as though it's the actor's holy grail. As with the myth of talent, I think the fixation on some elusive truth proves limiting—perhaps even a bit confusing—for students seeking to understand what goes into making a believable characterization. "Performances are lies," said Stanislavsky, getting right to the heart of the matter. It's much better to tell students, "You must make up a creative lie so convincing that the audience, the other actors, and you yourself believe it."

A creative lie is a complex fantasy often supplied by the author or a fantasy the actor creates that fits the author's story. Depending on how developed a supporting role is, the actor may have to be an imagined collaborator with the author to achieve a detailed creative lie in order to bring his supporting role to life. Therefore, to be an effective actor, you should believe in the lie in the same way you believe in an erotic fantasy that turns you on. Since you know it's all make-believe, you are free to imagine anything and be anyone the author wishes you to be, as you help to fulfill his story.

THE THIRD MYTH: THE USE OF THE WORD "CHARACTER"

The third great acting myth centers on the use of the word "character." Who is the character? As a young actor, I remember desperately trying to find "the character." It was always an elusive process. Where is he? Under the chair? In the corner over there? I nearly drove myself crazy. I thought I'd better read the play until all the happenings in the author's story began to affect me, just like they did when I was a kid reading Mark Twain.

I was eleven years old when I read *Tom Sawyer* under an old apple tree in Montville, Massachusetts. I remember falling in love with Becky Thatcher. For a while there, I actually thought I became Tom! However, I never needed to look for his character. He just popped out of Mark Twain's writing.

In creating a role, I never make a conscious decision about how I walk or talk unless it's a particular choice supplied by the author. Instead of trying to research and create details to "find the character," I spend my time reading and rereading the play or screenplay in order to absorb all that the author has written. Slowly the script starts to arouse my emotions and I begin the quest for the role, or as they say, "the character." The key here is to take what the author has described in an attempt to create a full-blown human being. I spend my time digging deep into the author's intentions to the point where I usually won't have to look for the "character"—it will more likely find me.

By understanding the limitations of the three myths, I have allowed myself the time through trial and error to create an unfettered, organic approach to acting.

CHAPTER 4
THE FIVE FOCUSES OF ACTING: AN APPROACH TO AN ORGANIC TECHNIQUE

The hardest challenge in making the transition from actor to acting coach was coming up with a way to verbalize the techniques I found useful in approaching the many roles I've played. Even though I had been acting for more than fifty years, it was extremely difficult to convey these techniques to another person. As I began to coach other actors, I started to distill and refine the thought processes and research skills I commonly used in creating a role. This gave birth to what I now call the Five Focuses: Your Reason, Your Objective, Economy, the Essence of Behavior, and Experiencing the Back-Story.

I never would have become an acting coach if not for encouragement from my friend and former agent John Crosby. In the late 1970s he represented several inexperienced actors who needed help in preparation for film and television auditions. At his request, I coached Jamie Lee Curtis, Rene Russo, and Sharon Stone, among others. Then, in 1982, when Crosby became Vice President of Casting for ABC Television, the number of students he sent me to coach increased dramatically.

Instead of relying solely on agents and managers to send actors to him, Crosby would take his keen eye to cover the broadest possible canvas—comedy clubs, modeling agencies, and even college drama departments in the hope of developing

TV stars for his network. These young actors and comedians were then sent to me for coaching; among them were Arsenio Hall, Mariska Hargitay, Mick Jagger, Heather Locklear, Chad McQueen, Larry Miller, Jack Scalia, and Alan Thicke.

Many of the students sent my way had little or no training, or were novice actors mired in confusing and mystical interpretations of the Stanislavsky Method. Most of these actors had lots of potential, and it was a pleasure to help nurture and develop them as they built their careers.

THE FIRST FOCUS: REASON

It's important that you carefully consider your reasons for pursuing an acting career. Take some time to think about your motivation for wanting to be an actor. The burning desire you feel is important, but it's even more important to understand what's behind that burning desire, what fuels it. If acting is simply disguising a desire to make a ton of money, then I'd suggest that you head to Wall Street.

Being an actor can be a drudge. Making a living as an actor is a miracle. The majority of actors need to rely on outside jobs to pay the rent. The Screen Actors Guild web site (www.sag.org) states, "Most SAG members earn less than $7500.00 per year from Screen Actors Guild jobs." Many earn nothing at all. Therefore, you need a powerful reason for wanting to be an actor. Self-knowledge will help you to stay clearly focused on your reason. By the way, I wouldn't trade my experiences as an actor, good or bad, for a huge pile of gold.

Stick to it. It may lead to directing, writing, being an agent, being a studio head, or just becoming a fine working actor. My daughter Marian is a very fine actor who does only socially relevant plays for a non-profit theater company. During the day, she has an important, well-paying job. After an early dinner with her guy she heads for the theater and acts, directs, and produces original plays. If, however, you find yourself at the right place at the right time with the right part that has your name on it, you may grab the brass ring and become a star. But you had better be ready.

Awareness of the reasons you became an actor in the first place can help enormously in dealing with problems that will inevitably crop up over the course of your career. All actors suffer through periods of low self-esteem. Actors are, for the most part, inherently reliant on others hiring them for jobs, so it's uncommon to meet an actor who's been at it for a while who hasn't suffered through dry spells when they wonder if they'll ever work again. If you know why you're committed to acting, those reasons will help you understand yourself and your work, and that knowledge should help save you from much torment. A solid, well thought out reason is your first focus.

THE SECOND FOCUS: OBJECTIVE

Many actors think the objective of acting is to give a good performance or draw attention to oneself. It is not. The objective of the actor is to help tell the author's story.

When the author wrote the script, he created a fantasy. Whether the story is about modern-day life in your own neighborhood or about people long, long ago in a galaxy far, far away, it's a flight of imagination created by the author. Thus, the work of the actor is to enter the author's fantasy and act it out the same way you act out your own fantasies.

I played the mayor of an ancient city that never existed in a Movie of the Week called *The Archer: Fugitive from the Empire.*

Without realizing it, most human beings are acting most of the time. It's a requirement of living in a civilized world. Suits, ties, and carefully applied lipstick are elements of the mask we all use. Even if you're in a terrible mood or feel sick when you show up to your workplace, you don't reveal it, you hide it with pleasantries and smiles. We pretend. Many times we are relying on our imaginations to just get through the day. As an example, consider your own sexual fantasies. When we are alone at night, with no books or movies on hand, the various details of a sexual fantasy can come together to create involuntary automatic behavior—sexual arousal. This is an aspect of the human mind common to everyone. Therefore, when an actor applies the details of the author's fantasy to his own imagination, he can create involuntary, automatic behavior, if he lets it happen.

I recently played the role of Papa in *My Sexiest Year,* once again using all the techniques described in this book. *Photo by Dan Littlejohn. Courtesy of MSY Productions, LLC.*

Automatic behavior is at the core of believability. Wonderful moments can happen when you immerse yourself into the details of the author's imagination.

Admittedly, this is easier said than done because our desire to remain faithful to the author's intentions is confounded by a human foible that all actors have within. Our egos want us to be "good actors" when we really need to stay focused on just doing the work, entering the fantasy, dealing with the details, and telling the story. It took me many, many years to overcome trying to be good and just focus on the work. Finally, it's always a good idea to ask yourself how well you think you've done your work.

THE THIRD FOCUS: ECONOMY

While you are on the stage or in front of the camera, you should never do anything that takes away from the story—no extraneous movement, no extraneous conversation, and no extraneous emotion. The actor's performance is simply needed to tell the author's story vividly, beautifully, and convincingly.

Imagine you're acting in a movie, and the director is framing the shot in a medium close-up. You start the scene with, "Get out of here, go away, I don't want to see you here anymore!" while flailing your hands and arms wildly at your fellow performer. "Will you please get the hell outta here?!"

"Cut," the director interrupts. "Will you stop using your hands?"

"Well, that's the way I talk," you respond.

"The story isn't about you!" the director continues. "It's about a guy who doesn't use his hands."

Film and television acting in particular demands a more subtle approach. Finger pointing and gesturing wildly with your hands is not economical, and the only thing people will see on screen is your exaggerated responses. It's much better to deliver the lines using your hands as little as possible. That way each gesture will carry that much more weight and be that much more effective when needed.

Once you begin to consider economy, it will be easier to control your hand movements, as well as other physical gestures that can clutter your performance. From the moment you step on stage (or in front of the camera), you must be aware of what your face and your body are doing.

Some actors are trapped by their own gestures. They say, "So long" with a wave of their hand, but then they can't get the hand down. It's stuck. Suddenly, the actor panics, aware his hand is raised, and yet he worries that he can't bring it back down without the movement of his hand becoming extraneous or distracting. The solution is simple: just put your hand down. This is what we do in life, so relax and the hand comes down. Less is more. So, do nothing that takes away from the story!

THE FOURTH FOCUS: THE ESSENCE OF BEHAVIOR

Since plays and movies attempt to portray a person's life in an hour and a half, everything in the drama should have vitality. In a well-written piece, all the details in the story are enormously important.

When a director says, "You need more energy," he really means the scene isn't important enough for you. If it were important enough, you'd have an abundance of energy.

So, if you're doing a part and it doesn't seem important for you, you better ask yourself why it is not. It's your job as an actor to make the author's fantasy—his written intentions—central to everything you put into creating your performance.

It's crucial in reading the text and learning your part that you find the essence of the character's behavior. Through study and rehearsal, you have to discover those elements most important to the story and make them the basis of your performance.

Be aware that the drama or comedy you're performing is a distillation of life, not life itself. Life has too many long, boring passages to be translated directly into drama; authors take life and distill its essence into the texts of their works. It's important to keep this in mind as an actor, and therefore give the action and emotions in a particular text their appropriate weight.

Let me use my performance as Grandpa in Neil Simon's *Broadway Bound* as an example of this process. Grandpa is a complicated, multi-layered role, and I found everything I needed to create the character in the wonderful dialogue and descriptions Neil Simon provides in his comedy. I read the play aloud, playing all of the parts. Not merely once or twice, but five, perhaps even six or seven times. Then, during rehearsal, I began to get on my feet and, of course, the director worked with us.

The first thing I did was to incorporate the dialogue I'd memorized with the movements we worked out in rehearsal. I watched the blocking to ensure I was never standing behind anybody. I made sure I could be heard and seen at all times. It sounds simple, but this process is basic to what we do. If the audience can't see and hear you, then go home and start another profession.

I then began to break down the play, scene by scene. I worked to discover what I wanted the audience to feel about me at each moment, and what I wanted the other actors to feel about me. In addition, I worked out what I wanted to feel

Me in *Broadway Bound* with Hildy Brooks, Jason Wolk, Alex Craig Mann, and Art Metrano. The play was at the Hudson Theater in Hollywood, directed by Gary Blumsack.

about the other actors, and what I wanted to feel about the story arc of the play as a whole.

Because I'd been raised in neighborhoods (the Bronx and Queens) not far from where the play is set (Brooklyn), the general attitudes and backgrounds of the characters were familiar to me. I grew up in the Jewish milieu Neil Simon depicts, so I didn't have to stretch a great deal in order to get there. What I had to do was understand in-depth, as much as I could, the relationship of this old man to all of the members of his family and to his history as Neil Simon describes it to us.

Once I'd done all that work to familiarize myself with the words and actions of the drama, it became equally important to incorporate all that preparation within the context of the performance itself. It's important that each time you give a performance, it's like the first time. It needs to be as if you've never done it before. To find the essence of behavior is to re-create the role each time, not merely reproduce it.

Many actors go down the wrong path because somehow, by accident, they give a good performance opening night (which can happen), but then they have no ability to reliably repeat that performance—it can't be done. If you try to reproduce, you're usually going to fail. What you have to do is re-create. The way you re-create is to go from detail to detail to detail. The author's fantasies can be created in the same way we use our own imaginary details to fulfill our sexual fantasies.

Examples of the Essence of Behavior

1. A love interest is the man or woman you always wished to have (so don't have sex with your leading man or lady, because you risk diminishing the heat of the love scenes).

2. If it's a mother you love, it's the mother you always wished to have, or father, or brother, etc.

3. The villain is the mythical person you hate the most—the epitome of villainy.

The epitomes of hate, happiness, love, etc., are goals to achieve through your imagination, the details of which result in the "essence of behavior," a useful tool for revealing the amount of importance given to each moment in each scene you're playing.

THE FIFTH FOCUS: EXPERIENCING THE BACK-STORY

Essentially, the back-story tells the history of what has happened to a character before he makes an entrance. Whether the back-story details events in the distant past or in the immediate moments before the actor comes onstage, it's probably the most important tool the actor has. It literally springs him into action.

A typical example of the sort of details many actors provide when they describe a character's history might go like this: "I was born in Chicago in 1960. My father beat me and my mother hated me. I went to school and the principal didn't like me either. My girlfriend left me, and I robbed a bank and I went to jail. Okay, I'm ready to act." These sorts of things are not going to do you any good at all. I've seen actors write out whole backgrounds for characters that were essentially useless.

A girl who plays someone who has been raped has to have been raped in her mind. She has to experience the rape in her fantasy, and I mean in every little detail. The guy who commits murder really has to commit murder in his mind. He has to do all the details of committing the murder. He has to experience the back-story.

For instance, in the opening scene of *Broadway Bound*, Grandpa enters holding a paper bag. Unbeknownst to the audience, the paper bag contains his soiled bed sheet from his recent nap. As he comes down the stairs, his daughter confronts him. Now if the actor does not experience the back-story in his imagination, he will not be able to fulfill the essence of behavior existing in the following details: Grandpa wakes up and recognizes that he's soiled his sheet. He feels embarrassment and pain; he feels alone, worries about growing old. He needs to experience all the elements of his back-story before he comes down those stairs and enters the action on stage. When I fantasized those moments immediately before entering the scene, I was automatically able to bring all the details of Grandpa's behavior into it.

I didn't have to go through every detail of his seventy-plus years, but it was important to fantasize the things I may have needed in order to spring onto the stage. I needed a full-blown Grandpa in my mind before I made my entrance—that included having previously worked out my relationships to his various family members in rehearsal.

The key to finding this back-story and bringing it to each performance is simple. As the Group Theater co-founder Harold Clurman always said, "Just read the play.

Everything is in the play." Each time you rehearse your words and movements you will make new discoveries—if you're open to them. Listen to the other actors. If they have suggestions, try to be ego-less in the process. If you are ego-less, you can listen to what everybody has to say and choose the suggestions you find valid. If you're egocentric and you're worried about how good you are, a useful suggestion may be interpreted as negative criticism. Take advantage of everything you possibly can in order to develop the role.

The back-story of the text is a very reliable framework upon which to build and refine your performance. While individual actors may have differing reactions to a character's back-story, over all they tend to be rather consistent, with perhaps slight variations. Let's do a little experiment. When I'm finished with this little fantasy, we'll see if your reactions to the back-story are the same as mine.

We are now going to create the back-story of *Hamlet.* Imagine you are Hamlet, Prince of Denmark. Your father is also named Hamlet. It's the 10th century. There are cobblestone streets and knights in shining armor. You live in a great big castle. As a boy, your father took you everywhere. He taught you French, Spanish, Italian, and English. He taught you to fence and joust. He imparted all his military and governmental knowledge. He taught you geography and history. You worshipped the ground he walked on. Your mother loved him and worshipped him. You worshipped her. You were a wonderful family. The lords and ladies of the kingdom loved all of you. Even the gravedigger was your best friend. You were sent overseas to college, where you excelled in your schoolwork.

One day, the palace messenger arrived and informed you that your father was dead. You were crushed. You cried yourself to sleep that night. The next morning, your friends carried you to a coach. You then boarded a ship and sailed for several days. After landing, you then took another coach and traveled for several days before you arrived at the palace. The people in the palace lowered their eyes as you passed them. You ran to your mother's room. You ran into her arms, but her arms were cold and in the room was your uncle, Claudius, whom you've always disliked. When your father was around, your mother never even talked to him. Later you found out that within a month of your father's death, your mother married your uncle. That night you find out that your uncle may have murdered your father.

You are Hamlet. On the space below, write down what you would like to do. Afterward, turn the page for my answer.

"KILL HIM."

Shakespeare doesn't let Hamlet kill Claudius. Without Hamlet's tremendous desire to kill Claudius, the play goes out the window. That's why the back-story is so important. The antithesis of *Hamlet* is the sitcom. Rarely does a sitcom author give the actor any back-story. Therefore, the actor must create a back-story that pushes him onto the set within the idiom of the story and with the result the director wishes to achieve.

While performing in the sitcom *Night Court,* I had to create a back-story just before my entrance. John Larroquette's character had been bitten on the ass by a neighbor's dog. I played the doctor who was supposedly administering to his ass off screen. The judge entered. From off stage Larroquette yelled, "Oh my God! Oh! Oh!"

The judge, thinking John was with a girl, said "oops" and began to leave. Just then, I entered and said, "You can have him, he's all yours." Big Laugh.

My dilemma was how I could convince the audience I was completely disgusted with Larroquette. I needed a solid momentary back-story that would spring me into the scene. I racked my imagination and finally came up with a wonderful off screen moment. I imagined that while I was bandaging John's ass, he broke wind right in my face right on cue as the judge said, "Oops." I bolted into the scene and said, "You can have him, he's all yours." It was a simple back-story involving a very unpleasant odor.

Often in sit-coms, the writers just tell jokes. You have to create the human condition out of your imagination. The same goes for bad plays and bad writing in general. On the way up, we take what we can get, but we do all of it as if we're doing *Romeo and Juliet.*

May I point out to you that imagining a fart did not require enormous talent or even any talent at all, just a little imagination and an understanding of experiencing a simple back-story that can spring the actor onto the stage.

CHAPTER 5
THE DISCIPLINE

Once you have attuned yourself to the Five Focuses, you are ready to take on "the Discipline." The Discipline is a technique in which you read the material you're working on out loud and allow your unconscious mind to make all the decisions. Once you've mastered the technique, you can take any book or any play from any shelf and allow your unconscious to do the work.

When you do the Discipline, you read the script each time as if you've never seen the text before. Glance down and read a few words, then look up and say the words without imposing any attitude or meaning. This way you stay as true as possible to your un-analyzed experience of the work. As you repeat the process over and over, you become all the characters as well as the audience. Moreover, if you continue to do the Discipline as you read the play, it will come to life for you just as when it's performed live for an audience seeing the story unfold for the first time.

It's very important for the actor to realize he can work by himself. He doesn't need a crowd of people, or a stage, or a set, or even a director to begin his work. Those things will be important later, but first the actor needs to do most of his preparation—most of his rehearsal—alone. He needs only himself and the text with which he is working.

READING THE TEXT

When you pick up a book and read the text, it's probably rare that you ever stumble over an unknown word. However, you can't read it if the book's written in Arabic, Hebrew, Latin, or any language you don't already know. The reason you can read a book in English is because most of the words are already in your head—you know how to say them and you already know their various meanings. The only time you'd read aloud badly is when a word comes up with which you're not familiar.

Have a friend open a book and randomly select a sentence short enough that each word can be spelled out one letter at a time. For instance, if I were to say the individual letters, "s-i-t d-o-w-n," you would respond by saying, "Sit down," because you understand how to use that phrase. You didn't impose anything on it or give it a special inflection, you just said, "Sit down." The important thing is not to interfere with the natural, organic way in which you would speak the words.

Simply allow yourself to absorb the words. Don't interfere with the context the author has set forth and don't allow yourself to interpret any of the words, phrases, sentences, or paragraphs. Just let the author's work sink in. Don't attempt to color it or impose your own ideas upon it. Most of all, avoid thinking about your performance as you read it.

MEMORY AND THE DISCIPLINE

Many actors have a great deal of trouble memorizing text, but thankfully, the Discipline is extremely helpful in memorizing the words of a play or script.

When you read the play for the first time, use the Discipline, but read aloud all the roles in the play. Doing so will allow you to become more and more acquainted with all the characters as the story unfolds, just as an audience would watching the play or movie for the first time. Do the entire play repeatedly. Soon you will find yourself doing more than one line at a time. At this point, you've begun to automatically commit the words to memory.

Aside from the benefit of memorization, the Discipline is a great tool to take to a cold reading in front of a casting director. Instead of having your face down in a script, you'll always be looking the casting director right in the eye as you say the lines.

Furthermore, the Discipline allows your unconscious mind and your instincts to do the acting without imposing an intellectual approach on the words.

REMEMBERING TO FORGET

The key to "remembering to forget" is to make it seem to the audience that you, the actor, don't know what's coming next. Despite your intense memorization, it should seem to the audience that you're spontaneously improvising the lines as you go along. It's as if you have indelibly written the script upon your brain by using the Discipline, giving each line and action its own organic and unadulterated treatment, just as you did the many times you read the play aloud.

When Hamlet says perhaps the most famous line of dialogue ever written, a line familiar to millions, "To be . . . Or not to be," that famous phrase should come out of

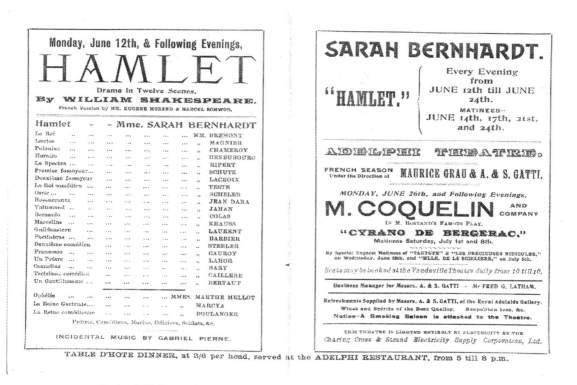

A playbill from 1899 in which Sarah Bernhardt played Hamlet.

the actor's mouth as if he's just made a great discovery of the alternative of "not to be," as if those words are being spoken for the first time.

In that moment you are, in a sense, writing the material even though you've memorized the lines. You want the audience to believe that your brain composed those thoughts in that precise moment on the stage. That's how you create a reality that will guide your performance from the inside—where the thoughts are generated—to the outside, where the words are spoken.

REHEARSING

When you're rehearsing a play, you should read the entire text every single day. Start by learning the first scene. Then, before going back to rehearse with the director and other actors, visualize yourself on the set with the other actors. Fantasize the scene in your mind so you can see all of the details of the scene; your speech, movements, interactions with the other actors, and even the set. All of this gives you another chance to evoke more details from your own imagination, to go beyond what the author has provided.

Conducting these fantasies in my mind has always given me a creative power I would not have without that preparation. Furthermore, I find that it heightens my sense of anticipation as I wait for the chance to bring my well-developed fantasy to life.

Then learn the second scene. That night or the following morning, before going to rehearsal, fantasize the first scene, and then fantasize the second scene, playing all of the parts. Learn the other actors' parts in the scene, so essentially when you're fantasizing it, you're talking to yourself. Moreover, be careful to re-create the play each time, avoiding the trap of falling into certain habits or a fixed performance. Try to discover it anew each time. Eventually you'll imagine the entire play in your mind.

Do the Discipline every day, before and after every rehearsal. You can do that at home, on a bus, on the subway, even in your car. You can record it if you want to but it's very important that you continue to rehearse all the time. Keep it as fresh as possible. This regimen of rehearsing doesn't end after opening night. Many second-night performances can fall flat when an actor tries to reproduce the excitement and energy that was a result of the weeks or months of preparation. Don't reproduce the performance—*re-create* it every time with all the tools of imagination at your disposal. Each performance, just like each rehearsal, be it alone or in the theater, is a chance to do the details and simply tell the story better than the author could have imagined. Don't expect to be a genius or to be a great actor. Just do the work.

Each time you fantasize, rehearse, or perform, allow yourself new discoveries. Each time you will grow and develop in the part. Stanislavsky said, "It takes as long to be good in a part as it does to have a baby." I don't go quite that distance, but I'm certain you get the idea. Practice makes (near) perfect.

FEAR OF MEMORY LOSS

A fear of memory loss is the actor's worst nightmare. What actor hasn't dreamt of the curtain going up and them having no idea what she's supposed to say, or even what play she's doing. Milton Berle, Raymond Burr, and even Marlon Brando all used cue cards, but if you're not a star, chances are you won't get cue cards.

Me with Milton Berle at the Friars in Beverly Hills.

If memory becomes a problem in your work, many courses out there can help you improve it. The techniques you'll learn will improve your work, not just by improving your memory, but also by giving you the confidence you need to know that you won't forget your lines at a crucial moment. I recommend The Memory Book: The Classic Guide to Improving Your Memory at Work, at School, and at Play, by Jerry Lucas and Harry Lorayne. It will improve your memory tenfold. Memory is a muscle that can be developed and strengthened.

"Watch yourself sleeplessly, for although the public may be satisfied with you, you yourself must be your own severest critic."
Mikhail Shchepkin (1788–1863) from *My Life in Art* by Konstantin Stanislavsky

Go through all of the various things we as actors do; use the techniques you are learning. Before you go on the set, question yourself: Will I be economical? Will I do the details? Will I tell the story? Will I find the essence of behavior? Will I experience the back-story? If each of these elements is brought forward in your work at each rehearsal or each time you read the play, you'll be able to have a barometer by which you judge your work. Keep in mind, the one critic that often eludes the actor is himself.

CHAPTER 6
DEVELOPING THE SENSES

Most of us touch, but we don't feel. We look, but we don't see. We sniff, but we don't smell. We eat, but we don't taste. We hear, but we don't listen. That's fine for the steelworker or secretary, but it behooves the actor to develop those senses in the same way a blind man develops all his other remaining senses. He touches objects and "sees" them with his fingers. His hearing is sharpened as he focuses on the sounds as if he has touched the sound with his fingertips. The actor must use his eyeballs like fingertips to develop all of his senses and explore the world around him.

The actor should also be able to see beyond the features of a surface and into the fine details. A simple snapshot is not enough. The actor should familiarize herself with every nuance of her environment. She should allow the total environment to affect her, thereby freeing her imagination.

Our five senses are how we take in the information of our world. In order to re-create a world on stage or before a camera, we must be able to simulate the information those senses receive while we're on a stage or a movie set. In those environments, there may be very little to stimulate our senses in a meaningful way. Unless we're on location somewhere cold, productions rarely provide sub-zero temperatures for us when we're playing scenes taking place in freezing environments. We must convince the audience that we are cold despite the heat of the stage lights. Again, I go back to 1952 while playing *Richard III* outdoors in Ohio. I spoke the lines, "It is now dead midnight, cold fearful drops stand on my trembling flesh," to a matinee audience at 2 PM on a sun-baked Sunday afternoon. I loved the challenge of that moment. The heat and the sun made my imagination stronger.

It is crucial that we learn to "record" this sensory data in minute detail before we get to the theater or soundstage. To accomplish this, try an exercise. Take a look out your window and try to see what is out there the way you would feel the landscape if you were actually touching it. Rather than recording the snapshots of life we usually collect when looking at the world, try to see more closely. Run your eyes over every centimeter of the view out the window like a blind person would run her fingers over someone's face. Feel the textures, contours, and even the colors with your eyes. Take note of how the shadows and light play across the surfaces.

Me as Richard III in 1952 (age 26). *Photo by Axel Bahnsen.*

When you look away, do you notice how your memory of the scene is much more detailed? Do the details of the scene stay with you longer? It takes a little practice, but you will find that if you start looking at things in this way, you will have a much richer store of knowledge and sensory experience to draw from when you're acting.

Now, try the same exercise with your ears. Listen to the noise on a street corner the way you would feel something with your fingertips. Pick out the different sounds and their sources and note the way they interact with each other. What's in the background? What's in the foreground? Listen for every tiny sound. Try the same thing while listening to a piece of music. Feel the music's movement, the changes in volume, tempo, instrumentation, key. Try to hear the musicians' fingers on their instruments.

Next, try the same thing with your nose. Walk around your house or your neighborhood and just focus all your attention on your sense of smell. What scents come and go, which are stronger and which more subtle? Do any of the scents trigger memories? In human beings, the sense of smell isn't necessarily weaker than in our animal cousins, it's simply that we use it less. Our sense of smell is closely linked to our memories and emotions.

Finally, work on your sense of taste. Rather than gulping down your dinner, really take the time to taste it. Focus on the flavors that fill your food. Most dishes consist of combinations of ingredients, so try to taste them individually. Once you've delineated all the different flavors, notice how they combine.

All this sensory work involves is seeing, hearing, smelling, tasting, and touching in three dimensions. In the process of going through our daily lives, we have a tendency to flatten out our perceptions, to take in sensory data in only two dimensions, noting only what's pertinent to us in that moment. Every detail of an actor's environment becomes important. Each detail's relationship to the other details is also crucial. So, as you go through your everyday life, try to retune your senses so they fully take in all the information bombarding us throughout the day. After this data is collected and recorded in your brain, it will be there for you to recall during your performances and allow you to create a higher level of reality in your imagination and in your work.

CHAPTER 7
HISTORY AND STUDY

Points of view without the benefit of history hang like sheets in the wind, flapping and unsupported. In acting, as with any other art form, we should be aware of what has gone before and be acquainted with the body of knowledge accumulated by the old-timers. Read and study the words of these past masters to establish a sense of the history for the craft you have chosen. You will find this short quote as relevant today as when it was written in 18th century (the complete quote is in Book One of *Actors on Acting*):

[Acting] ought to be ranked amongst the learned professions; for the truth is, that in order to be a good actor, there is required a greater share of genius, knowledge and accomplishments, than for any other profession whatever; for this reason, that the profession of acting comprehends the whole system of human life.

(James Boswell (1740–1795), "On the Profession of a Player," from *The London Magazine,* 1770)

Just as the actor needs to study other disciplines, above all else he needs to study his own craft. Many actors claim not to study acting for fear of losing their "natural" gifts. This is ridiculous. Perhaps they're simply afraid of discovering how much they don't know. Nonetheless, whatever "natural" ability you have will not evaporate because you study acting. Study will help you gain new and often useful techniques.

> "He who claims to teach Art understands nothing whatsoever about it."
> *Eleonora Duse*
> (1858–1924) from *Antologia del grande attore*

Beware: Not all acting teachers are created equal. An acting teacher or coach who is helpful for another actor may not be helpful to you. Investigate, read their books, sit in on a class before you invest yourself too heavily. Some people learn more from a one-on-one session than they do from a class. Seek out impeccable credentials, but most importantly find someone who loves teaching. They're hard to find but well worth the effort.

Studying the history of acting must continue throughout your career. Again, much of our history is contained in one wonderful book, *Actors on Acting.* It captures the breadth of the history of acting. The knowledge and experience it contains is invaluable. Here's an example: Laurence Olivier wrote, "If somebody asked me to put in one sentence what acting was, I should say that acting is the art of persuasion. The actor persuades himself, first, and through himself, the audience."

Eleonora Duse. Artwork by Sid Maurer.

CHAPTER 8
CONTRAST AND CONFLICT IN COMEDY AND DRAMA

Contrast and conflict in theater, television, and motion pictures are important for the structure of the play and certainly for the enjoyment of the audience. In the middle of *Macbeth*, just before Duncan is murdered, Shakespeare turns the spotlight on the gatekeeper, who functions, really, as comic relief amidst all the dark doings.

Shakespeare creates an enormous sexy, funny comedy scene just before the murder. This contrast allows the audience a break from the bleakness of Shakespeare's tragedy. It also serves as a counterpoint, which heightens the dramatic action just ahead.

If you place a white square in the center of a group of gray squares, the white square will not stand out. It will blend in with the other squares, and may take on some of the grayness of the squares around it.

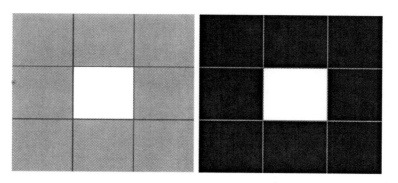

A graphic example of contrast. *Graphic by David Rickett.*

However, if the same white square is surrounded by black squares, the contrast will make the white square stand out brilliantly.

Similarly, in order for an actor's performance to stand out boldly, he or she must always be aware of the contrasts found throughout the script, at every point in the story. Without attention to these contrasts and conflicts, the performances and the play are surely lost in a muddle of lukewarm choices.

In the great silent film *City Lights,* Charlie Chaplin as the little tramp is in a rich friend's Rolls Royce. He sees a lit cigarette butt lying in the street. He stops the car and delicately picks up the butt, takes a puff, gets back in the car, and speeds away. He creates a wonderful comedic moment emphasizing the contrast between the wealth symbolized by the Rolls Royce and an action we would naturally associate with the impoverished little tramp.

Chaplin also uses contrast to hilarious comedic effect in *The Gold Rush* when, on the verge of starvation, he boils and then eats his shoe as if he's eating a filet mignon. He makes his point (he's starving) and creates wonderful comedy by playing the extremes of emotion and behavior. He's so hungry, he literally eats his shoe, but he eats it as though he's dining at Delmonico's! Again, unexpected contrast makes the scene that much more effective.

There are many other examples of contrast and conflict, and the actor has to prepare in order to make the most of each one. King Lear, in opening the play, must clearly be happy as a baby that he's giving up all his cares to his children. He's eager to be free from his royal worries and is beaming with pride at the daughters who will succeed him. Then he asks each one of his daughters to tell him what they think of him. The two eldest tell him what he wants to hear—both Goneril and Regan are glowing and tell him wonderful things, making him prouder and happier still. Then he looks to Cordelia, the youngest and his favorite; however, she disappoints him when she bluntly declares her love for him without flattery or embellishment. From that one action, Lear goes from the highest high to the depths of torment—from absolute ruler to absolute beggar—and it's the conflict and contrast inherent in his tormented journey which drives the remainder of the play.

Contrast, a difference between light and dark, and conflict, the emotional highs and lows, are the essence of good drama and good comedy. The actor must be aware of these intrinsic elements at all times.

An old comedian is on his deathbed. He's fading fast when his son comes to him. The comedian says, "I'm dying, son."

The son, full of worry, says, "Is dying hard, Dad?"

The old comedian summons all his energy and replies, "Dying is easy, son, comedy is hard."

This old joke certainly rings true. Comedy is serious business for the actor. Elements such as timing are extremely difficult to teach. More often, actors have a knack for it, something innate—but you *can* learn to do comedy, and more importantly learn to do it well, if you pay attention and allow yourself to feel what is happening in the moment. Too often on sitcoms (and in bad movies), we see actors who are doing little more than waiting to deliver the punch line. Such an approach to comedy instantly kills whatever humor was present in the writing.

It's important for the actor to play comedy just as he would drama. The actor must take the action of the scene very seriously and deliver the lines just as he would were he performing in a straight drama: keeping everything in mind, his objective, the essence of behavior, and the back-story. Economy is even more critical in comedy than in drama. If the actor thinks he's funny and mugs for the audience, he'll surely flatten out the humor.

The essence of comedy usually comes from the situation. If the writing is funny and the situation is funny, the actor just has to be involved in the situation. Moreover, if he's deeply involved in the situation, the humor will emerge.

> "The worst is when all is quiescent in art, all in order, definite, legitimate, when there is no need of argument, struggle, when there are no defeats, hence no victories either. Art and artists must move forward or else they will move backward."
> **Konstantin Stanislavsky** (1863–1938) from *Stanislavsky's Legacy*

In a play called *Jakobowsky and the Colonel*, I played a Nazi. I played him with a German lisp. In one scene, I came on stage and saw a man holding a gun to another man's head. I asked him, "What's wrong with this fellow?"

The man with the gun replied, "He has an obsession."

I then asked the fellow, "What is your obthethon?" delivered in the outrageous lisp. I always got a big laugh. It was crucial that I not try to be funny. I knew that if I thought about the line—and the lisp—and tried to say the line in a funny way, I'd fall on my face and miss the laugh. "Don't try to be funny, just play it straight." Playing it straight, fully involved in the situation, the scene played very funny. It got laughs because the situation was funny. All I had to do was enter the author's fantasy and say his words.

LEARNING ON THE JOB

During an episode of *The Fall Guy,* starring Lee Majors, I co-starred with a famous Canadian actor. In our first scene together, my line to him was, "You drunken bum, if you don't stop drinking, I'll fire you."

The actor, who knew the script, seemed to take my reading personally and for the rest of the day ignored me. The next morning I knocked on his dressing room door. The door opened and he stared at me disdainfully. Finally, he said, "What do you want?"

I said, "I've got a great idea for our next scene."

He responded, "I hope it's a lot better than your other scenes, because you really stink."

I was hurt. Several responses went through my head. Should I clip him? Should I report him to the producer? Well, thought I, I shouldn't punch him as he's a much bigger man than I am, also he could report me to SAG. I could report him to SAG, but that would only make me look foolish. Therefore, I think I'll cry and tell him how much he hurt my feelings. That's what I did. The actor hugged me and told me he didn't mean it and how sorry he was.

During our next scene, he was so distraught he blew fifteen takes. This time I threw my arms around him and calmed him down. Therefore, at times it's better to go to hurt before you go to anger. The mystery of his strange behavior was revealed later when I found out he was a serious alcoholic and took my reading to heart. Now, as a result, I always go to hurt before I go to anger.

I was in an episode of *Baretta* with Ray Bolger, best known as the Scarecrow in *The Wizard of Oz.* (He had a long career as one of the finest musical comedy stars on Broadway and in movies.) I played Ray's manager. Unfortunately, we appeared in a scene with a miscast actor who kept going up on his lines. I became impatient with him and made a snide remark. The miscast actor seemed to take my insult quite well; however, after the take, Ray took me aside and in a quiet but stern fashion said,

"Allan, we must be the most supportive to miscast actors. It's not their fault and there's no need to hurt them. The world cries out for kindness, especially from us actors."

That was a very special lesson for me, and for all of us. Ray's gone now, but his words remain with me—and hopefully with you.

Me with Ray Bolger on the set of *Baretta*.

MORE MEMORABLE HAPPENINGS

One of the most fulfilling experiences I ever had took place on the Paramount lot in 1981. I had the privilege and pleasure of working with Jessica Lange in the film

Me with Jessica Lange in *Frances*. Photo by Gemma La Mana Willis.

Frances. It was the last shot of the day. My character, Mr. Bebe, the studio head, was admonishing Frances Farmer for her non-cooperative attitude. After three takes on my close-up, the director, Graeme Clifford, said, "Allan, on the next take, I want you to pinch her cheek and call her 'tootsie.'" That piece of direction was so conceptual, creative, and very idiomatic to the period, I immediately knew it would tell the story perfectly. I couldn't wait to do it.

Here I am taking direction from Robert Redford in *Quiz Show*. Photo by Nick Taylor. Photo courtesy of Hollywood Pictures. *QUIZ SHOW* © Disney Publishing Worldwide.

Immediately after the take, Graeme smiled and checked the gate with the D.P. (director of photography) and said, "Print it, that's a wrap." Although I realize it was a short scene in a big picture, for me it was an emotional high. I got into my car and cried with joy all the way home. It was an example of a shared creative moment of creativity between an actor and his director. Sometimes small moments generate big happiness.

Another wonderful example of an actor and director working closely occurred in my first scene in *Quiz Show.* As my character was exiting his office, the Rob Morrow character bragged he was with the congressional committee. I turned and looked at him, said nothing, and then exited. Robert Redford, the director, said, "Cut. Print that." I thought for a moment,

Ralph Fiennes and me in *Quiz Show*. Ralph is an inspiring, well-trained English actor who went from playing the brutal Nazi officer in *Schindler's List* to an intellectual college professor in *Quiz Show*. Photo by Nick Taylor. Photo courtesy of Hollywood Pictures. QUIZ SHOW © Disney Publishing Worldwide.

and before we moved on to the next setup, I called out to Redford and said, "Bob, I think I have a better take in me."

He answered, "I liked that one." I turned away, feeling I had missed the proverbial boat. Redford turned back around and said to the crew, "Stop everything, I'm gonna give Rich another take."

This time when Rob Morrow said, "I'm with the congressional committee," I paused and ad-libbed, "Congratulations," then I exited.

Redford said, "Print that, and Allan, anytime you want another take, just ask." Redford is truly an actor's director, one who identifies deeply with his fellow actors. There is a reward for having the courage and timing to speak up for yourself.

RESEARCH, RESEARCH, RESEARCH

The first time I played a judge, I spent two weeks at a courthouse soaking it all in. I observed the various judges, their habits, movements, decorum, etc. I read Witkins' *California Criminal Law*. Research always helps the fantasy feel authentic.

This is me on the set of *Bicentennial Man*, my second film with Robin Williams.

In the 1977 Movie of the Week *Tail Gunner Joe* (the story of Joe McCarthy), I played the counsel for the House Un-American Activities Committee, Ray Jenkins. I researched his whereabouts, called him, and spent quite a while talking to him on the phone. I asked him about everyone on the committee and all about Joe McCarthy. I also asked his permission to record the conversation. I was able to capture his essence—speech patterns and all—and I was able to incorporate much of Ray's persona into my final performance.

January 1996

In Francis Ford Coppola's film *Jack,* starring Robin Williams, I played Dr. Benfante, the guy who delivers the baby in the opening scene. When I was preparing for the role, I called an OB-GYN friend of mine, who arranged for me to witness a delivery. The doctor who completed the delivery spent a great deal of time with me before and after the birth teaching me how to hold the newborn infant and handle the baby in its first moments of life. Fortunately, he used a doll. I spent several intense hours with the doll going over his directions repeatedly until I got the feeling of being an OB-GYN.

When I arrived on the set, I had to handle a real baby. Had I not spent those hours in research I would have been a very confused and frightened actor. After the shot, I looked up and there were the mother and father, beaming, complimenting me, and asking me if I was a real doctor. That was the best review I ever received. Research will deepen your fantasy, strengthen your feeling of reality, and help involve the audience in what's happening.

Me with Gloria DeHaven.

December 1996

Another example of research paying off was when I was cast in *Out to Sea* with Walter

Jack Lemmon and I on the set of *Out to Sea*.

Matthau and Jack Lemmon. I was to play the part of an archaeologist specializing in Mayan culture. The role consisted of two scenes, the first of which had two speeches. Since I believe there are no small parts, I prepared for my first scene by purchasing a book and tape on Mayan history. I read the book and listened to the tape once a

Me with Walter Matthau.

night for over a month. I'm sure I knew as much about Mayan culture, at that point, as many history students.

When I got to the set, the director, Martha Coolidge, said, "Allan, we need to cut back and forth between you, Gloria DeHaven, and Jack Lemmon, so can you ad-lib about the Mayan culture?" I proceeded to do five minutes on the amazing Mayans.

Research pays off.

THE SPIELBERG EXPERIENCE

March 1997

"Hello—Allan? It's Ginny Raymond, your happy agent. I just received an offer for you to be in Steven Spielberg's new film, *Amistad.*"

"So don't lose it," I replied. "I don't care about the money as long as I get my billing."

"There's no problem with the screen credit. And you got a two-week guarantee."

"Good," I said. "It's a chance to work with a master."

For the next few weeks, I read and reviewed the material, going several times to the libraries. First I went to Beverly Hills and then to the main library on Fifth Street in downtown Los Angeles. It was there that I found several books on the slave ship Amistad. I filled myself with the period, created the back-story for my character, Judge Andrew T. Judson, and did forty or fifty takes in my head.

Before I knew it, I was on an American Airlines flight to Boston, where a car and driver met me. I shared a ride with David Paymer, whom I'd worked with in the film *Quiz Show.* We chatted until our arrival at the Marriott Hotel in Newport, Rhode Island.

We were soon informed that our call time for the following morning was 4:30 AM. Rhode Island is freezing in early March at any time of day, let alone 4:30 AM, but who cared? I couldn't wait to begin working with Spielberg.

The next morning I found myself at base camp. I had a beard, but the hair and makeup artist instructed me to chop it off, leaving prominent muttonchops or large sideburns. "No, let's ask the director," I said.

"Okay," she replied, as she proceeded to put on my makeup. A little eyeliner later, my makeup was done. However, as simple as that was, my costume proved to be much more complicated. There were tights, knickers, a frilly blouse, and a massive black robe. At least it was warm.

I asked to go the set early so I could have plenty of time to get acquainted with "my" judge's bench—including my gavel, papers, books, and other props—and, more importantly, to meet and make friends with the prop master, the director of photography, and the various assistant directors.

Soon I was introduced to Mr. Spielberg himself. He was very open and friendly and I tried to express how pleased I was to be there. I then began discussing my beard, saying I wanted him to see it so he could make the decision on muttonchops.

I played Judge Judson in *Amistad*. Photo by Andrew Cooper. Courtesy of Universal Pictures. AMISTAD © Universal Pictures. All Rights Reserved.

"No," he said, "I have complete faith in my people—so whatever my hair and makeup person says, she knows the period better than I do. If she said muttonchops, start chopping."

Quickly, my beard was off and I was left with the muttonchops. Most importantly, I was also left with Spielberg's philosophy: A man is only as good as the people around him. Each member of his crew—from the production assistants to the director of photography—is the best at what he or she does.

The special effects and set people transformed the surrounding area of the courthouse to 1839, with wagons, horse-drawn coaches, and people dressed in 19th-century garb. All the details reflected the period flawlessly. The interior of the courtroom was just as impressive. Soon, all the extras dressed as townspeople paraded into the courtroom. Then the actors playing the slaves entered. Many of them had been brought over from Africa and didn't speak English; they spoke authentic dialects. The general atmosphere was open and full of love and enthusiasm.

The first assistant director, Sergio, quieted everyone down and Spielberg began the rehearsal for the master shot. There were over one hundred people in the room, as well as ten to fifteen more outside ready to enter. Spielberg began to place us according to his vision for the opening shot. Since he knew exactly what he wanted, what is normally a painstaking process took only fifteen minutes. Janusz Kaminski, the director of photography, finished setting the lights while Spielberg completed his staging, and we were ready. Spielberg said, "Let's shoot it," and we were off and running. That day I got to work with Morgan Freeman, Pete Postlethwaite, David Paymer, and a young Matthew McConaughey. Needless to say, I got a big kick out of being in a Steven Spielberg film.

CHAPTER 9
STRUGGLE, SUPPORT, AND SUCCESS

STRUGGLE

All of the performing arts require extensive struggle in order to "make it." During the summer of 1978, I had the good fortune to spend an afternoon with the wonderful Bette Davis. While we were chatting away, Bette said, "Allan," pausing to puff on her cigarette, "what do you think is the most important thing about acting?"

I immediately shot back, "To master it."

"No," she snapped. "It's to make it. And Darling, I MADE IT." Indeed. She was a model, a bit player, and a star, not to mention a big troublemaker and mother. She was the head of her family and took care of everybody. She fought for better parts and changed her screen persona as

Sylvia Kristel, one of the greatest faces ever to go in front of a camera and one of the bravest people I've ever known. *Photo by George Hurrell.*

99

needed. She wasn't afraid to get old, and boy did she make it. She is a role model for all of us.

SUCCESS

If we achieve what other people believe to be success and we feel we don't deserve it, then are we actually successful? NO! Only if we believe we deserve success do we really achieve success. Therefore, to achieve success we must feel we deserve it; we've worked for it, struggled for it, sacrificed for it. Success is something we try to accomplish all of our lives. It's the result of an expertise we've strived for, one in which we have a consuming desire to achieve.

Since I'm speaking of the desire to be an actor, let's look at the different definitions of success regarding the way we feel about our work, leaving personal and family success alone for the moment.

Worldly success: That is when other people believe we are successful, i.e., fame and fortune. It is when the actor registers on a culture's gauge for success.

Personal success: It is a feeling within the actor that he has achieved an expertise and feels he has learned his craft. This is when our work is satisfying despite our continued struggle to achieve more.

Total success: That is when worldly and personal success is flowing hand in hand and we have achieved success in other people's eyes as well as our own.

We all need success at one time or another. Few of us can be content with personal success. Most of us, even if we feel personally successful, have a burning desire for worldly success. For us performers it is much more difficult because a modicum of worldly success is required for a career in a profession that can't be accomplished alone in a workshop or studio. Some audience recognition is necessary for us to continue.

Vincent van Gogh knew he was a great artist—as did his brother and many of his peers—but he sold only one painting during his short life and never could support himself. Modigliani and Soutine died of deprivation. Painters, writers, and musicians hope the public at large may one day discover the work they leave behind.

Perseverance is required for any success, but personal success in our hearts can sustain us while we strive for the worldly success. Therefore, don't wait for the phone to ring—make it ring. Remember, acting is ultimately a business.

SUPPORT

Actors, writers, and directors have a desperate need to be together. Every time a strong group of us has gotten together it has resulted in great theater: Shakespeare's Globe Theater, the Moscow Art Theater, the Max Reinhardt Theater, the Provincetown Players, the Group Theater in New York, to name a few.

The Group Theater offers the perfect example of the power of a creative group of actors, writers, and directors with a total support system. To be a member of the Group Theater in the 1930s was to be envied. From that support system came many of the major acting stars of the period. Fine actors, writers, and directors appeared on the international scene, some making lasting impressions: John Garfield, Lee J. Cobb, Luther Adler, Stella Adler, Frances Farmer, Uta Hagen, Franchot Tone, Morris Carnovsky, J. Edward Bromberg, and on and on. Playwrights such as Clifford Odets, Tennessee Williams, Sidney Kingsley, and Arthur Miller all began their careers as members or associates of the Group

> "Yes, I can see my own painting coming along, and I shall urge every man who comes in reach of me to produce; I will set them an example myself. All this, if we stick to it, will help to make something more lasting than ourselves."
> *Vincent van Gogh*
> (1853–1890) from *Complete Letters of Vincent van Gogh*

Group Theater member Lee J. Cobb (1911–1976). *Artwork by Sid Maurer.*

Luther Adler (1903–1984). *Artwork by Sid Maurer.*

Theater. Directors such as Elia Kazan, Harold Clurman, and Bobby Lewis and plays and motion pictures like *Men in White*, *Awake and Sing*, *The Country Girl*, *Dead End*, *A Streetcar Named Desire*, *All My Sons*, and *Death of a Salesman* all emerged from that support system engendered by the Group Theater.

The prerequisite of a working support system is the presence of respected peers—people whose ideas inspire us, who love us, and whose mutual respect we cherish. That is why actors, writers, and directors who can't find solace and support among their peers seek that support from agents and managers. Unfortunately, only highly successful actors, directors, and writers can receive service by agents and advice from managers. The artist's level of representation is in direct ratio to his value in the marketplace.

To find such a support system, the actor must find a buyer, like any good salesperson, the product being the actor himself. If you're a beginner, or even a professional without representation, walk, run, or drive to the nearest theatrical bookstore and get the books listing agents and/or managers. Compose a convincing cover letter and résumé, accompany them with a current headshot, then mail out five per day, wait a week, and follow up with calls to each place you contacted. In every major city there are agent and casting director showcases. Get a partner and a great scene that's right for you, rehearse the hell out of it, and showcase it. Try to capture it with a video camera. Remember, you're trying to break into show *business.*

There are alternatives to commercial show *business,* namely, regional theater. If you're lucky enough to become part of a permanent company, you might just make enough money to get by. In addition, there are community theaters everywhere—

groups of people who wish to produce, direct, and act in plays owned by the community. In America, actors in community theater require a day job so they can make a living and are free to rehearse and perform at night.

ACTING AND PSYCHOTHERAPY

Every stage of life is important, but it is those first few years that imprint lasting impressions on our psyche. There are no perfect parents; hence, there are no perfect people. Some of us had worse upbringings than others had. Some of us overcome adversity better than others do. We are constantly being changed, being challenged, being hurt, being uplifted, and learning lessons. This is why spending time in psychotherapy can be a

Me with Meredith Dallas and Allyn Moss in the original play *Hear Ye*. Meredith Dallas was one of the greatest actors I've ever worked with. I did many plays with him during my three years at Antioch. He always remained in Yellow Springs, Ohio, even though his ability, looks, and behavior could have taken him to the top. He stayed at Antioch teaching and acting while raising his wonderful family with his beautiful wife, Willa. *Photo by Axel Bahnsen.*

great help to the actor who must make creative and business choices that balance into a life that's right for you.

It is important for actors to gain as much insight as possible into what is happening within their lives and personalities. The best way we can accomplish this is by relating our experiences to an objective person well trained in the sphere of psychology and psychodynamics. With the help of the therapist who understands our experiences, we can begin to analyze them and come to gain insight and understanding regarding the impact they have had upon our current personality.

The emotional and psychological defense mechanisms we create as children don't necessarily carry us through adulthood. This can result in a whole list of difficulties that affect us not only as people, but also as actors. Fear of failure, stage fright, butterflies, and inhibitions can all be manifestations of unexplored experiences from our past. Professional help can develop the insight to break us out of these patterns; without help, many of us unconsciously indulge in destructive behavior that may prevent success or turn success into failure. I've spent some forty years delving into the various aspects of my own personality because at a young age I knew that something was going on that was not particularly good. I would say a large percentage of my success as a husband, as a father, as a member of society, and as an actor can be credited to the work I've done with psychotherapists. Many of the therapists didn't work for me, but I never thought the practice of psychotherapy was wrong. I kept delving into myself, searching for answers as to why I was who I was, and how I became that person. At the beginning, I sought relief from emotional pain. When the pain left, I discovered a world of creative ideas and insights.

This is a portrait of me painted in 1953 by my longtime friend Sidney Maurer. I think he captured my pre-analysis angst quite well.

How does this relate to your work as an actor? Once the individual begins to understand himself, he can better understand others. We all face the death of loved ones, disappointments, desires, joy, and the full gamut of human emotions. Before psychotherapy, many people think their problems are unique, that what has happened to them never happened to anyone else. The truth is that all of us have to face enormous difficulties at one time or another.

The actor who lacks insight is limited and doesn't have the tools to handle the various conflicts in life. The revelations and the insights discovered in psychotherapy become invaluable tools.

I often quote Shakespeare when I'm depressed, or in a difficult emotional state. "To be or not to be . . ." is a very insightful speech, and if one really understands it, and breaks that speech down line by line, the psychology that Shakespeare intuitively understood is remarkable.

For actors, I recommend a very revolutionary therapy called *psycho-imagination,* practiced at the Psycho-Imagination Institute in Los Angeles by Dr. Joseph Shorr and his associate Dr. Jack Cannella. (See reading list below.) It works much the same way you work as an actor—through your imagination. This particular psychotherapy relies on fantasies that are presented to the patient, and when the patient goes through these fantasies and talks through them, it gives direct insight into his unconscious; like a Rorschach test, except it produces much clearer results. In experiencing these fantasies, the essence of the person is released, and he or she can make enormous gains as to what's going on in his or her personality. The practitioners of this therapy are not gurus, they don't present themselves as parental figures, but rather as people who are experts in their field who can make their knowledge useful to the patient. Furthermore, since the institute is non-profit, psycho-imagination is less expensive than other therapies.

Many students have come to me with apparent psychological problems. However, since I'm simply an acting coach and a fellow actor, I wasn't about to psychoanalyze them. I recommended they seek help. In many cases, it helped make the difference between success and failure.

I recommend the following books, which will give you exposure to this new psychotherapy:

- *Go See the Movie in Your Head* by Dr. Joseph Shorr
- *Our Inner Conflicts: A Constructive Theory of Neurosis* by Dr. Karen Horney

- *Neurosis and Human Growth* by Dr. Karen Horney

If nothing else, these books will be useful in your work as an actor. Therapy is not a cure, but rather a tool to obtain a better understanding of who we are, what we are, where we want to go, and how we get there. What better investment can we make than in ourselves?

CHAPTER 10
SOME LETTERS FROM STUDENTS AND CASTING DIRECTORS

THE STUDENTS

Over the years, I have asked many of my students to write a paper about what they have learned in order to find out if I have reached them. The following are examples from the papers I have received—some short, some long. Many of my students have explained my acting technique a hell of a lot better than I can. Perhaps it is because they are younger and better writers.

I recommend you look up these actors and casting directors on the Internet.

Pete Antico of *We Care About Kids*

PETER ANTICO ON THE ORGANIC APPROACH

Allan Rich's organic approach to acting focuses on how outside stimulus has a direct effect on human behavior. He would tell me there was something hanging on my nose and then watch

107

my reaction. Without thinking, I would react by wiping my nose. When I looked in the mirror, to my surprise I had nothing on my nose. I would say to Allan, "You lied to me."

He'd respond, "Exactly, and you fell for it, hook, line, and sinker. You see, my dear boy, actors are creative liars, and I got an organic response from you." From that moment on, I was hooked.

When an actor goes on the stage, he has three huge obstacles to face.

1. The actor must create an in-depth back-story, detail by detail, to make himself believe he is the character he is portraying. In a sense, the actor is lying to himself about who he is. The more detail he creates in his background, the more believable his character becomes. (Great con men do this).

2. The actor must go on the stage in front of an audience who already know they are seeing a make-believe situation, with actors who are obviously not the people they are portraying.

3. The actor must then make the audience believe they are watching reality when in fact they know it is only a play and not all the characters are real.

What a fucking dilemma! Many acting coaches beat you over the head with the statements "Find the truth in the character. Acting is about the truth. Find the truth." Is there really any truth?

When you really think about it, the truth in any character is nothing but a creative lie—a totally fabricated, made-up back-story. The actor must believe it, commit to it, embrace it, and love every molecule of it. Is that the truth? Or is it the actor believing the fantasies he has made up (back-story) and embracing his lies as the truth?

If you are playing King Lear or Hamlet, and you are obviously not King Lear or Hamlet, how then do you justify the truth? You were not born in the century of those characters. If you say you found the truth in playing those characters, you had to lie to yourself about who you were in the past to get there. You must believe your lies with your heart and soul so that you become them.

If you believe in yourself, other people will also. That is true in all aspects of life. People love to believe a man with conviction.

I believe great actors are great liars. All of them! Pacino, DeNiro, Nicholson, Streep, Hopkins, Daniel Day-Lewis. And I am not talking about parts close to the actor's own human experience, where you can just show up and say the words and you need little or no back-story. That would be mediocrity and not much of a personal payoff.

I am speaking of playing characters that are far and sometimes nonexistent experientially to an actor. Now that's exciting. It is a space where the unexpected and the unforeseen are borne into existence in the moment your listening is so powerful that you have no other choice but to embrace the present and react to the outside stimulus that surrounds you. Life is fired at you from point-blank range. Magic happens.

Great writers write in detail. Allan taught me that an actor's job is to act out the details of the author's fantasy. And if there weren't enough details, create them. Always do your back-story, then simply LISTEN and RESPOND. If you do a scene repeatedly, the key is to RE-CREATE every take by listening powerfully so that you are completely present in the moment and your listening will create your own organic responses time after time after time.

Allan has said that the closest you can get to the greatest literary minds in the world would be to READ their work. Tolstoy, George Bernard Shaw, Chekhov, Dostoevsky, Ibsen, Odets, Tennessee Williams, Mark Twain, and William Shakespeare, to name but a few, are some of my friends now because of Allan.

Acting as a craft is a gift that lets you embrace all different kinds of humanity through the characters you play. The more you know your craft, the deeper the embrace. Actors are truly ambassadors of humanity. Roberto Benigni's performance in *Life Is Beautiful,* Bob DeNiro in *Raging Bull,* and Jose Ferrer in *Cyrano de Bergerac* are great examples.

Well-trained actors are craftsmen. They have their own barometer to judge the work they do. Either they act out all of the details or sometimes they miss a few. Nevertheless, the well-trained actor always knows exactly how he performs. When someone else critiques him, beware. He will always know who is trained in the craft and who acts by accident.

When an audience watches an actor that really knows his craft, they say it's magical. Allan, thank you for all the magic you have given me.

Thank you for the privilege of studying with you and teaching me how to be an ambassador to humanity.

Love and Respect,

Pete Antico

HOW I FELT AND WHAT I LEARNED

a paper by Mike MacDonald

Introduction

I have this meeting with John Crosby at ABC and he says, "Call this great acting coach." So what am I going to say, "No, fuck you?" So, I call. I get to your house, I'm led into a small room, and I'm told you're going to be an hour late. $400.00 and the guy's late. I see your picture with Ted Kennedy and I'm relieved to find out that you are who I thought you were. I start to watch some tape of a guy named Harold Clurman. I'm not too thrilled, but two minutes into the tape I'm intrigued. (Later when I told

Me with Senator Ted Kennedy.

my girlfriend, she filled me in on how important this guy was.) Soon I'm told to watch another one. In the middle of that you come in, there's a brief hello, I continue to watch the tape. I finish and you give me another tape to watch. I finish and you give me some reading material to go through. I start to get a little uneasy in the fact that we haven't said more than a few words to each other.

Finally, you come into the room and begin to talk to me. I already had respect for you by being familiar with some of your work. You then continue your session with me by trying to discourage me by saying stuff like, "I haven't had much luck with comics."

That's okay, because after about 30 minutes I guess you think I passed because you open up the flood gates and my mask comes down and we fly. Three hours later, you hug me and I get into a cab.

How I Felt

After meeting you, I went back to the place where I'm staying and phoned my manager and my agents and simply said, "I've found my acting coach. He's cool. He's in."

You have no idea what a breath of fresh air you are compared with my first attempt at finding an acting coach. In Toronto, someone suggested I phone this bitch named Loy Coots. She made me feel like a boy with no hands who wished to paint the Mona Lisa.

You can see why I think she's a bitch. Loy Coots made me feel like a dirty rag. A worthless comic who could never get into the magical, exclusive, and predestined country club of the almighty actor.

I think Loy Coots is insecure, not satisfied with her own career, and therefore afraid of the flood of people who will pass her. It kills me how Loy Coots couldn't teach me one thing, whereas, if I never see you again, you have taught me already things I will keep with me for the rest of my life. I felt with you a complete confidence that if I apply myself there is no stopping me. All the things you said made sense to me. I have complete faith in you as my coach. I also like you as a person. You revealed to me that you have a sense of humor and compassion for life.

Not only have you opened the door that Loy Coots slammed in my face, you have placed a ladder in front of me that stretches to infinity. I can climb as high as I want and you will steady the base until I am clearly on my way.

What I Learned

I learned that I can apply myself, and the only thing that will stop me is my own lack of desire and sense of dedication.

The "steps of focus" are concrete, clear-cut, and something I can sink my teeth into.

Reason: "To help bring people closer together." I think this is the best reason to be involved with any form of the arts and entertainment.

I would like to have moments in film as Meryl Streep had in *Sophie's Choice* when she had to choose which one of her children would die. When I first saw this film, I was so completely lost in the story. I feel that artists have the responsibility to make people feel, react, think, laugh, cry, to dream and basically WAKE UP!!!!! Bring people closer together if you have to drag them kicking and screaming!

Your Objective: "Tell the story." It seems so simple. Just tell the story. Don't think, do. I've found this to work in the auditions I have been to already.

Economy: "Movement which only helps to tell the story." I was happy to see this as a step of focus because it is something that really bothers me about these new "character comedians," who twitch and lunge around the stage, their movement having nothing to do with the joke.

An example of this is Robert Duvall in *Tender Mercies,* as opposed to anything by Jack Klugman, an actor caught in a parody of himself, doing the same gesture every time he is on the screen. Sometimes when you watch early films of older actors today, you see a presence, an energy that I guess like a plant, sometime during their career, they just stopped watering, and it ceased to grow. Looking at the "Brat Pack," the new actors, a lot of them are like flowers with no roots. Economy of movement is something I will have to work on constantly.

Essence of Behavior: "The epitome of behavior"—something I was not aware of but it seems straightforward and practical. Using the scene in *Sophie's Choice* as an example, it is obvious that if Meryl Streep didn't really believe that, first, the children were her own and that, second, one of the them would never be seen alive again, the scene would not have been so powerful.

Knowing this step and applying it to any scene will certainly make it more believable. Let's say I was in a movie about a man's torment of going through a divorce. Now how could the audience relate to my pain unless in the first act I convinced them that I really loved my wife?

Back-Story: "History of the character, leading up to the scene." I was aware of how important this was in writing scripts. Sometimes experiencing the back-story becomes the first act. Your example of experiencing the back-story when you played the doctor amputating his own son's leg was very clear and understandable.

In application, the audition I had for the Ernie Kovacs character that comes home late from the studio and spoils his family's plans for a trip, experiencing the back-story really helped the scene. So, thank you.

The Discipline: I think the more I do it, the more I will see and understand how the play and the people evolve like osmosis. I've applied it already in situations where I go to a general meeting and they ask me to read something cold. Using the Discipline has proven very effective. Most casting people's reactions are, "Very good reading. Very natural delivery." I think it probably stands out because everyone else tries to "act" the scenes, imposing too much on every line.

Another very important thing I've learned from our first meeting, and especially our session to help me with the two auditions I had, was the importance of details. Seeing the details of a scene helps so much in the acting of it. The breakdown of each scene we looked at was so illuminating to my sense of how to approach it.

In essence, I think everything I've learned from you is like the difference between a gladiator going into an arena with a blindfold on and one going in with a sword and shield. The proof is in the pudding: 7 meetings. 3 call backs. 2 "You're the guy we're going to pitch." 2 "Let's put it on tape." 2 "Very good reading." 3 "We're going to find something for you to do." And 3 "I want some other people to see you." I am batting a thousand.

I'm very pleased at the way things are coming. I feel my money is well spent. Thanks for the sword and shield, "coach."

My gratitude, my best,

Mike MacDonald

First Step . . . Samuel French

Second Second Step . . . Life!

(or Vice Versa)

by Denise Loveday

My initial meeting with Allan Rich was one I'll always remember.

After sharing introductions and telling Allan my personal background and acting experience, he had me watch a video of his late acting teacher, Harold Clurman. Well, by the first few minutes of the tape, I had goose bumps all over. I felt like I had "come home." That's the only way to describe it. Oh, what it must have been like to actually *know* and *work* with this wonderful man! I immediately felt that if Allan Rich subscribes to Clurman's philosophies, then I'm headed down the right path.

Then I was shown tapes of Allan's own TV/film performances, and in short, I definitely liked what I saw. His performances were rich in detail and personality without being phony or overdone. Getting his message across, he was direct and simple. Then I saw an old tape of an actual acting session he had with a new student of his. I knew immediately that I wanted to learn from Allan.

The last two hours of this energizing day officially became my "first acting lesson" with Allan Rich. He had me read a few articles, including one he had written on conquering inhibitions and being open to spontaneity. I gobbled this article up. Someone was finally addressing the bottom line for me. In past acting classes, the coaches would say, "Be open! Get out of your way! etc." But no one told me how! I needed a "technique." With Allan, I got a taste of the answers I wanted. He mentioned Herbert Ratner, saying, "Go from moment to moment like building a house. Create the framework." Then Sidney Kingsley had told Allan, "Identify with the character and just do the *details.*" That was it. I wanted to hear more!

I wish I'd had a tape recorder going to capture all that we talked about. Allan asked me *why* I wanted to act and he said, foremost, we need to remember our pure love of sharing human experiences and feelings with our audience. All the rest is secondary: the fame, fortune, or feelings of approval that we may be seeking (from, say, a parent or significant other).

We have to be dedicated to our art and to learning. We, as actors especially, should read *constantly.* Read anything and everything we can get our hands on: plays, classics, fiction, newspapers, etc.

And most of all, we have to be open to life and realize that life does not revolve solely around acting.

Next, we discussed Allan's FIVE STEPS TO FOCUSING for a scene:

1. Be clear about your reason for acting. Act for the pure joy and love of sharing human experiences and emotions with your audience.

2. What is your objective? Read the scene and enter the author's daydream. "Do the details," by committing to the author's daydream. Feelings and automatic actions will occur. Preplanning or imposing certain emotions upon the scene will cause you to push. Trying to impress will also cause you to push. Don't try to impress— to be good. It's not about being good. It's about going back to step #1 and your strong desire for telling the author's story and touching the audience.

3. Don't add any unnecessary facial expressions or body movements. Remember to just tell the story. Don't clutter.

4. Remember that all scenes can be reduced to love and desire. For maximum conflict and emotion, always raise the stakes. The more you have at stake, the more you fight for it, the harder you can fall if you fail.

5. Be clear about your character's "back story." Use details that the author supplies. Make up and take the time to *experience* in your mind your character's past. Experiencing a rich character history will mean a richer "front story."

Finally, we reviewed Allan's method for reading a play. While sitting, look down, "pick up" the line in your head, look at the person you're addressing, pause, and say the line as naturally as if you just made it up yourself.

I left Allan's house that day with my assigned reading list in my hand and my head racing. So much to think about! So much of it made sense and I was excited knowing that I only had more ahead of me to absorb and discover and learn. As I learn more about acting, I'll learn more about myself *and* life. Or is it the other way around? The more *I* open up to life and it to me, the more I can embrace acting with all the heart and knowledge I so desire. "Either way," I eagerly thought to myself, "right now, it's off to Samuel French Bookstore!" And that's just where I headed.

A MESSAGE FROM LARRY MILLER

To Whom It May Concern, To One And All, To Anyone Who Wants To Live A Creative Life:

People ask from time to time what my first big break was in show business and

Larry Miller.

I tell them, with complete sincerity, that my fist break was the day I decided to do it. I tell them there is no such thing, really, as a break the way most people think of it. The moment I thought, "I want to be an actor, a writer, and a comedian," that was my break, the only one I needed, the only one anyone ever needs and the one that's always available, like faith, to anyone who has the clarity and the meekness to ask for it.

This rarely satisfies them and often makes them think I'm holding back or that I just don't want to aid them. I can't help that. My problems are (1) trying to be a good father and husband and (2) being the best artist I can be.

Every so often, however, I meet another brother, a seeker, an artist, who as part of his great abilities is also a helper and a teacher. I don't think I'm one, but I know one when I see one. Allan Rich is one. He's a great actor, and, coincidentally, just the other night I saw him again in *Quiz Show.* The life he radiates, from without and within, through craft and instinct, made a character who is both awful and understandable, which is not only compelling, but in its banality, more horrifying than Frankenstein. He has done this many times as an actor, and it makes him a great artist, but he can also bring others along. Not to it exactly, to that place we can only bring ourselves, but he points at it and leads, guides, and nurtures, and his concept and technique, the leap from the Method, is a very, very good idea.

You know what his best lesson is, through? The smile on his face. No kidding. The first time I met him, and he smiled, he lit the joint up. That's why I like hearing the guy's voice, too. Even when it's frightening, it's still, somewhere, full of light.

Aw, hell, I guess I just like the guy.

FROM ALAN THICKE

With my background as a writer and talk show host, I knew I was ill prepared when called to audition for a new sitcom called *Growing Pains.* In a panic, I sought out the best teacher in town, the unanimous consensus being that Allan Rich was the guy I needed. Allan quickly sensed my groveling with trepidation in his presence and recognized a frightened would-be actor completely intimidated by the prospect of facing a joyless horde or network executives for my audition.

He offered the simplest and most sensible approach—to find a part in myself and perform said part with the confidence and conviction that accompanies me day to day, person to person, job to job. He pointed

In Robert Redford's *Quiz Show* I played the President of NBC, Robert Kintner. Photo by Nick Taylor. Photo courtesy of Hollywood Pictures. QUIZ SHOW © Disney Publishing Worldwide.

Alan Thicke.

out that there are few roles requiring an actor to create something totally outside of his realm of experience and familiarity, and even fewer actors capable of pulling it off. Allan gave me the assurance that somewhere inside me was the character I would need to find for the role and that a version of who I really am would probably do nicely.

I performed the audition with pride and confidence, presenting the part of my personality that evolved into Jason Seaver and gave me a good life. I can never thank Allan enough.

WORKING WITH ALLAN RICH

by Linda Porter

After an absence of many years (30, to be exact), I was free to reenter my first profession, acting. I knew I had to "sharpen my axe." An actor I trusted recommended Allan. My eldest son had studied with him and thought highly of him.

In his luxurious Hollywood Hills home, after meeting Allan, his wife, Elaine, and their two adorable Lhasa Apsos, Charles and Lily, we began our work together. My career began in radio at age eight and in the theatre at ten, but I had taken a long hiatus to raise a family. Who knew if what I had considered as a magical time, a mystical connection linking the work and me and the audience, would still exist? In our two or three private sessions, I gained a growing sense that not only would the connection reappear, it would be strengthened tremendously. As a child, enraptured with this wonderful game of jumping into another existence, work was literally play. Now, the structure behind the magic was revealed. It was exciting and challenging. The sessions were filled with art from Allan and Elaine's magnificent collection and literature and videos of Allan's work to illustrate points he was making. (I remember Allan's requirement that each of his students read a large number of the classics, but since I'd already read all of them, we discussed a few and went forward to how art related to the arms race, the blacklist, etc. We were on the same page there.) In addition, there was always wonderful food.

Soon it was time to enter Allan's Actors Workshop. I met his other students, all much younger than me, each of them capable of amazing work. We'd be assigned a scene (from a large carton of them), read them once to feel the details popping out, read them together, memorize them, and perform them an hour or two later with simple blocking, props, and costumes, on a set of our invention in front of Allan and the other students, after which a post-mortem was held. It was tremendous fun! The results were amazing. Because we had all received the same training, we were on the same page, and could truly zoom ahead. What a time it was. Friendships blossomed which have never died.

Allan is a genuinely kind person and generous to a fault. When I felt ready, he had an agent for me to meet. At least one of my early credits (a "MOW" [Movie of the Week]) was a result of a recommendation to the director. The confidence I gained from my work with him was priceless. I've never looked back. It's been twenty years since those days. I work a great deal, in TV, film, and theatre. I have a wonderful life. Somewhere in my memory bank, easily accessible, are the glorious memories of those hours with him and my mates in the workshop. What heaven!

Thank you, Allan. Love, Linda

FROM MAGICIAN WHIT HAYDN

I started out as a street performer in the late 1960s in New York, and eventually moved out to Los Angeles in 1975.

I met Allan around 1979 at a private party where I was performing. After watching my performance, he came up and said he thought I had a lot of talent, and wondered if I had

Me with Whit Haydn, Close Up Magician of the Year 2005 at the Magic Castle in Hollywood (and great at parties).

ever studied acting. I told him I had not ever really had any formal training, and as we talked, I became more and more interested in the theory of acting as he presented it. Soon I was taking private and group lessons with Allan, and was totally fascinated. My study with Allan informed my magic in many ways. My comedy and character became more defined and more integrated. It was easier to construct new routines and to develop unique character presentations both in stage performances and in more intimate "close-up" magic venues.

Allan gave me a theoretical system that helped me in creating and stylizing a performance piece and also in analyzing where I might be going wrong when something didn't seem to be playing right. When I was performing at a peak level, I was able to "own" that work and to repeat it time and again without losing that special spark.

Allan was able to teach me that without training, performing as an actor, comedian, or magician is instinctive and "accidental." It is easy to slip from great to bad when the audience or mood breaks your concentration. You can be a great performer some nights for some audiences and flop on other occasions without knowing why.

With Allan's help I was able to develop critical judgment about my own work, and to understand what I was doing that I should keep doing, and what I might need to change. I have to give Allan credit for taking my performance from the broad comedy and course acting of the street performer into a much more subtle and refined sort of comedy based on character and situation.

Me with Rene Russo. By the way, that's the costume I wore in *Night Court*.

This has had a huge impact on my career, and for his kindness, wisdom, and knowledge I will always be grateful.

RENE RUSSO, ACTRESS

Allan introduced me to the craft of acting. He inspired, educated, and encouraged. I shall be forever grateful.

TOM MUSTIN, NEWS ANCHOR, DENVER, CO

Allan Rich is an actor's actor. An acting coach without peer. For years I had wallowed in the darkness of acting theories and techniques. Allan helped me see the light.

DIANA BARTON, ACTRESS

Never before have I been so honored as to be asked to write a letter about one who has guided my life as you have.

When I came to you, so long ago, I had just begun my journey in life. I was so young (seventeen I think) and I am sure I told you that I knew everything there was to know about acting, life, and anything

Tom Mustin, actor and news anchor.

else you asked me. That's a lotta nerve from a kid from Palm Springs who grew up with big dreams and big tumbleweeds blowing by. You taught me how incredibly important it is to listen and discover the magic of simply telling the story. I have used the tools you taught me all through my life. I have lived the part of being an outsider; you said most artists feel this way. I never forgot the day you used that word to describe me. I felt so home.

I can never fully comprehend what being blacklisted was for someone of your talent. I can only tell you of the impact you have made on me and the joy I find in our friendship. Keep it up.

Love,

Diana Barton

NO LONGER AN ACTRESS BY ACCIDENT

A Paper on Focus and Enlightenment

A Rebirth Due to the Awareness of the Psychological Technique

By Didi Alan

To say I had been waiting a lifetime to hear your technique is an understatement. No words can express the exalted joy and sense of recognition I experienced upon hearing your words.

You've stated that your objective is "to assist the actor in rediscovering, through the stimulation of awareness, knowledge the artist has blocked from his conscious mind because of past doubts and personal insecurities which have rendered him creatively impotent."

I have been crippled, searching for simple truths to unlock and free my creative spirit. To say I had been ignorant or unaware would be an injustice. A more accurate appraisal would be to say I had forgotten (as if in a deep sleep) basic elemental truths and concepts I instinctively knew. I needed to "hear again" and rediscover these "truths" in order to be reborn.

It is said that everyone has a double, upon meeting whom there would be instant recognition. I recognized this psychological process as if it were my own, my double. I felt as if a mirror had been placed against my soul so I might see all I had lost sight of.

Vision and understanding is a gift which frees not only the creative, but the whole being. I feel as if I have been given back to myself, and like a young child, can begin to grow.

Who are you? You are the direct result of every one-celled animal and plant that was on this planet when time began, a result of all the combinations of genes in your family.

It is in my genes to be creative. You've stated, "People who are artists by nature, whose behavior has succumbed to False Gods, feel in their hearts they have behaved against their wish to produce art and are left with frustrated negative feelings they don't understand and that cause them mental pain."

I was searching, studying, and longing for the "truth" which would help unlock my creativity. I thought I didn't know what the "truth" was but would recognize it when I heard it. I was frustrated, disillusioned, and depressed.

Actors know that the hardest part is getting out of the way of themselves, and teaching establishments are very big on promoting this concept. However, nobody will show you HOW! Coaches will say, "Leave your problems at the door," or "Get out of the way of the character," but NO ONE (in my experience, until now) will show you a process by which to do it.

When I heard the technique, I knew my search for truth had ended. I recognized the key that could unlock the passage through which my creativity would flow.

The Psychological Technique and Steps to Focus

Your reason. To help bring people closer together. Assume their problems and let your own fall by the wayside. A good actor must have a good reason and be full of will, not just want to satisfy his parents or because somebody significant in his life didn't know he existed. Your reason gives you your will.

Your objective. Tell the story. Find out what the author's daydream is and enter it, just as your own. The details will create automatic involuntary behavior. Do the details of what is going on and the feelings will come. If you tell yourself how to respond, you'll inhibit yourself. If you try to impress, you will push. Thinking gets in the way; just do the material.

Economy. No superfluous movement or facial expressions. Use only movement that helps tell the story.

Essence of behavior. Romantic love: In every boy and girl, there is the epitome of love—for the girl, the knight in shining armor; for the boy, someone to shelter and protect. (Example: The more open the girl is to "him," the more vulnerable she can be as an actor.) The more you love or desire something, the harder the fall can be. Therein lies all contrast, drama, and the epitome of behavior.

Back-story. This is the entire history of the character leading up to the point of the scene. You are the result of your own back-story, everything in life up to that moment. The whole back-story must be experienced in the mind and be carried to its logical conclusion. It must be so vivid that the front-story is rich and full of life.

In addition to these five steps, there is "the Discipline," or a method of reading a play aloud and entering the author's fantasy, his situation, circumstance, and period, to allow the play and the people to evolve like osmosis.

Talk the way you would talk normally and do the details as you see them. You allow the rivers to flow between the words, and remember how to forget your next line. The Discipline teaches you how to listen and enables the script to become "your mind."

So what does all this mean?

Prior to this point, I was "acting by accident," and knew it. I was scratching the surface and just "getting by." When complimented on a piece of work "well done," I felt fatuous and undeserving. I knew I hadn't done the work, but wasn't even sure what needed to be done. I knew in the very center of myself that acting was an art form which deserved the same amount of study and hard work as required to become a doctor or an accomplished painter or musician—if not more. I didn't know what to study, which books to read, or even how to begin.

I gave away the bride at Didi Alan's wedding.

Your technique, substantiated by the masters, is a revelation to me. Understanding "in theory" will be nothing compared with the joy of hard work and concentrated effort put into practice on a daily basis; a process that will not only enrich my art but my life as well, for they are the same.

To quote Stanislavsky, "An actor is a teacher of beauty and truth. For this an actor must be above all, a cultured person, be able to pull himself up to the level of the geniuses of literature."

Thank you, for opening the door.

Didi Alan,

July 1, 1985

Finally, read a segment from on of my most recent students, Jesse Erwin.

UNLOCKING THE TRUTH

A paper about finding one's intentions

by Jesse Erwin

My Introduction to Allan Rich

Growing up, my mom would tell me that the best actors in the world were absolutely crazy and that they could take themselves to places where very few could go, anytime and anywhere. My first and most vivid memory of Allan Rich's acting technique took place in a make-up trailer, in a cemetery, on Veteran and Wilshire in Los Angeles. It was about five in the morning and I was sitting in a chair next to a girl about to be made up. Out of the darkness, an elderly gentleman named Allan Rich came stepping into the trailer in a dark suit, top hat, and big smile on his face.

Walking straight past me and up to the pretty girl, of course, Allan says with a great big smile, "Good morning. Are you ready for the big scene?" Before she even answers, Allan's facial expression changes, his eyes begin to well up with tears. He glances over at me and then back to her saying, "Now, when you go to do your scene today, and you see his dead spirit wandering about (pointing to me), you have to let the tears well up first, hold it, and then let them fall." With this, Allan blinks and his tears begin to fall down his face. He then looks at me with teary eyes and asks, "You got it?" Not knowing how to respond, I froze. Allan's smile returns and he sits down complacently in his chair and gets "made up." I remember thinking to myself, "Jesus, this old man is f@*$% nuts!" I was enthralled. I had just seen everything my mom had ever talked about in the course of 15 seconds.

I waited a long time to get the chance to have Allan teach me some of his techniques for acting. Moreover, today, I consider myself privileged not only to have had such an opportunity, but to have him as a friend as well.

Unlocking the Truth through the Psychological Technique

It's funny: Your whole life you are told to be honest, never lie, tell the truth and you will be rewarded for your good deeds. Then suddenly, you are thrown into a casting agent's room where he/she gives you a giant dragon suit, a script, slates you, and tells you to "make it real." How can one make that real? How does one find truth in that?

I was intrigued when Allan began to explain his psychological process as a means to create truth amongst lies. I learned that we all have within us creative answers to most of the things we are asked, and the difficulty comes in trying to find a way to unlock it. Allan Rich's psychological technique has taught me that through physical and mental awareness of one's outside stimuli, one can create an environment wherein involuntary human behavior, organic response, and discovery emerge. In other words, if an actor can manufacture a strong enough lie within which to believe with all conviction, a creative truth will unfold from it. So how does an actor unlock his or her creative truths? Allan has taught me the art of the creative lie as a means to unlock the truth. He gave me simple steps, a psychological technique, to help the actor rediscover himself through awareness and stimulation.

In order to convey truth in a creative lie, an actor must envelop himself in a back-story. A true artist must be able to develop a completely fabricated story about his/her character, believe in every single element of it, and embrace it like it was his/her life. It is important for the actor to do this because every single thing that he or she tries to do after that is a direct result of the back-story he/she has created. Thus, the actor becomes a living, breathing result of every piece of the creative lie up to that moment.

When the actor has created enough to commit honestly to his/her back-story, it will exist in the subconscious mind, finding its way out when it needs to. Then, the actor can focus on the "objective."

The actor's objective is how the actor creates himself in accordance with the writer's vision, and what they themselves have created through back-story. The more detailed and consumed the actor becomes with what is being asked, the more organic and spontaneous the actor will become in each scene, no matter how many times the actor is asked to do it. By heightening this awareness, involuntary behavior flows from the actor. To quote a friend and former student of Allan's, Pete Antico speaks of the excitement and magic that supervenes when the process is applied correctly. He said that by creating all the details well enough, and then listening intently and reacting honestly to outside stimuli, you'll find "a space where the unexpected and the unforeseen are borne into existence." That is the "magic" we actors try to bring forth—the ability to create something exciting that you did not even know was there by simply being in the moment.

Many actors seem to think this can be achieved by heightening one's mannerism. If a character is mad, he must shout and pull out his hair in a scene. If an actor is sad, he crosses his arms and makes a face to go with the feeling. Nevertheless, after watching Allan's reel, or any great actor for that matter, the most powerful scenes are when the actor is able to get his point across without any extra, inessential gestures or facial expressions. I can tell you firsthand that when my parents would look at me calmly and tell me how upset they were with me about something, it was a lot more powerful than when they'd yell. The same holds true in acting. An actor must watch his/her "economy" in each scene. In acting, and especially in film acting, less is more.

The only time actors should go that extra step to get their point across is when it helps add to the climax. Something important Allan expressed to me, and I have noticed in his work, is that there should be intent behind every action a character demonstrates. Allan calls this the "essence of behavior." If a character chooses to make a strong physical gesture to help fulfill his feeling, it should be employed only to set his character up for a final pay-off. Otherwise, it comes off as superfluous and detracts from the scene instead of giving to it.

With all these things to focus on and be in tune with when approaching any type of story, scene, or character, the most important part of Allan's method is the very first step.

That step is an actor's "reason." Every actor must have a good reason for wanting to do what he or she does. An actor should do what he/she does out of the love for human behavior and all its intricate parts. It is hard to assume a character's traits while fully allowing one's own to take the back seat. Moreover, one cannot assume the problems of other characters if he or she is too focused on his/her own inane ones. Nevertheless, if you have good reason for practicing your craft, your art, then the rest will fall into place.

The first day of class, Allan asked me if I believed that only some people were born with natural talent. I said yes, and he told me that I was wrong. He said, "Every person who is born and able to function within society on a daily basis is born with natural talent. But there is a difference between the people who spend one hour a day on their craft, or eight hours a day perfecting it." I thank you, Allan, for making me want to perfect my craft, and making me feel there is no reason any of us can't be as good as we strive to be.

What separates the good from the bad is not talent, but a willingness to put forth the extra effort. You have made me want to educate myself with everything from reading and writing to the study of human behavior (acting). There are not enough hours in the day to get to all the things I enjoy now because of you. I thank you from the bottom of my heart for taking the time out for me, and giving me pieces of information I will keep for a lifetime.

With great reverence,

Jesse Erwin

THE CASTING DIRECTORS

While you are at Samuel French or Larry Edmund's Bookstore, get a recent book on all the casting directors in your city: commercial, theatrical, and motion pictures. Sometimes they may be more accessible than the agents. Send a picture and a résumé, accompanied by a short letter about who you are as a commercial product. Keep in mind that it is a business, and the casting directors want desperately to discover a star. Find out their birthdays and send cards. Also, send holiday cards.

Always remember that casting directors are rooting for you. They cannot get you the job, but they can get you close. So don't go for the job, just tell the story and have fun. After all, a reading is another chance to ACT. If they like your work, they will call you in again, so just make friends. The following are letters from a few casting friends whom I love. Besides being wonderful people, guess what? They hired me.

Gloria Monty, Former Executive Producer, *General Hospital*

Just a short note to let you know how much I appreciate all the wonderful work you are doing in training actors. When I look at a résumé and see "trained by Allan Rich," I know I have a potentially fine actor in front of me. Your method of teaching has broadened the scope of the acting profession.

Mark Malis, Former VP of Television Casting, Universal Studios

I know Allan Rich as an actor and acting coach. I feel he exemplifies the best in both professions. His method gets results quicker than most acting coaches do.

Jennifer Shull, Casting Society of America

Thank you so much for giving your valuable time so freely to the CSA Minority Acting Seminar. It was a great advantage for students to be able to study with an actor and acting teacher of your caliber.

John Crosby, Former VP of Casting, ABC Entertainment

Allan is whom I highly recommend to any actor. He has a gift and shares it brilliantly!

Jane Jenkins, Casting Director

A Leap from the Method serves as a wonderful primer for young actors. Allan's approach to acting and the "biz" is simple and straightforward—one I always find the best.

Joseph D'Agosta, Casting Director

I am inspired by your love of acting, gushing out of each page of your book. The simplicity and innocence knocks me out.

Robert L. Joseph, Producer

Rich,

After finishing your book, I asked God whether I could live my life again.

'G' said: Why?

I said: Because I just read Allan Rich's book.

'G' said: Call me back in a week.

I said: Why?

'G' said: It's been a frantic week. I haven't quite finished it.

I said: What do you think of it so far?

'G' said: I'm jealous.

Bless you, Allan Rich

(Robert had a large body of work as a writer and producer on Broadway and the London stage and in films and television.)

Me with Robert reciting Shakespeare at each other.

CHAPTER 11
CONCLUSIONS

Giving back to the community is the best thing I do.

Back when I was conducting acting classes, I wanted to demonstrate how quickly we humans could change our feelings and outlook toward the world. I did an improvisation of a story I had in my head, playing all the roles. One of my students, Pete

Antico, understood the demonstration very well and suggested I write it as a script for a short film. From then on after each session, he would annoy me about writing the screenplay. Finally, just to end his constant harassment, I wrote the damn thing and handed it to him.

Not long afterward, Pete raised a substantial sum of money to have the script produced into a short film. I came up with the rest of the money and we produced *A Little Tailor's Christmas Story*. The story is set in a small

I played Shiller in *A Little Tailor's Christmas Story*.

neighborhood of Nazi Germany when everyone's ethics and morals are being put to the test.

When we showed the fifteen-minute film to a class at Hollywood High, the film emotionally moved the students, as well as Dr. Jeanne E. Hon, the principal. With Pete as a partner, we formed We Care About Kids Inc., a 501 C3 non-profit company, in 1994. During the past 13 years, we have produced, directed, and acted in seven socially relevant short films.

Two of my favorite people in Hollywood are Carol Gustafson and John Crosby. Photo by A.J. Matis, Jr..

We are thankful to stars like Maria Conchita Alonso, Cuba Gooding Jr., Carol Gustafson, Russell Means, Zack Norman, Willard Pugh, Madeline Zima, and Curtis Armstrong, who have appeared in our films along with many of my former students, like Kari Gibson, Patrick Smith, Larry Cord, and Linda Porter. My thanks go out to two former executives at Paramount, namely John Goldwyn and Sherry Lansing, who have donated space

Irish dramatist George Bernard Shaw (1856–1950). *Artwork by Sid Maurer.*

and theaters. John Farrand and Panavision have donated camera packages for shooting. I thank them for their kindness and empathy for the children we try to help. I spend most of my free time working gratis for the organization. Our lawyer, Robert Young, is a member of our board, as are Pete Antico and I. We all work free of charge. We all give back. So look us up at www.wecareaboutkids.org.

I hope the lessons and experiences I have shared with you in the preceding pages have brought you greater understanding. I would particularly recommend reading the complete essays from which the sidebar quotes in this book were taken. Shaw, Stanislavsky, Duse are all geniuses of the past. Study their words as a monk studies scripture. Much of their meaning lies beneath the surface and they will inevitably point you to deeper truths.

Remember, you are out in the world and experiencing life. These experiences and observations will fill you with ideas and knowledge and give you ample resources from which to create your work.

Finally, practice your craft constantly. Unlike me, I hope you don't make the mistake of turning down small parts. Do everything you can to take advantage of the skills and knowledge coming to you in each day's experiences. You will be amazed at how your work will grow and change the more you practice. Moreover, do not forget to be attuned to the people you are working with. Other actors, directors, writers, and technicians can all have valuable things to teach you.

William Shakespeare (1564–1616). *Artwork by Sid Maurer.*

Do not be afraid to be influenced by other actors. Inquire about their technique if you find it interesting. One of the greatest painters in history began by copying other greats. Vincent van Gogh spent many years replicating the styles and techniques of masters like Rembrandt, Delacroix, Gauguin, and others. It took him years to discover and develop his own style. Even though he sold only one painting in his life, he knew he would someday be a great painter. So, create a body of work wherever, whenever, and however you can.

You have the ability to be any kind of actor you choose. It's entirely up to you. If you possess the desire to be a great actor, you *can* achieve it.

In closing, I offer this excerpt from Shakespeare's *Hamlet* as a final piece of encouragement as you pursue your acting career.

HAMLET EXCERPT

HAMLET: Speak the speech I pray you, as I pronounced it to you, trippingly on the tongue: but if you mouth it, as many of your players do, I had as lief the town-crier spoke my lines. Nor do not saw the air too much with your hand, thus; but use, all gently: for in the very torrent, tempest, and, as I may say, whirlwind of your passion, you must acquire and beget a temperance that may give it smoothness. O, it offends me to the soul to hear a robustious periwig-pated fellow tear a passion to tatters, to very rags, to split the ears of the groundlings, who, for the most part, are capable of nothing but inexplicable dumb-shows and noises: I would have such a fellow whipped for o'erdoing Termagant; it out-herods Herod: pray you, avoid it.

FIRST PLAYER: I warrant your honor.

HAMLET: Be not too tame neither, but let your own discretion be your tutor: suit the action to the word, the word to the action; with this special observance, that you o'erstep not the modesty of nature: for anything so overdone is from the purpose of playing, whose end, both at the first and now, was and is, to hold, as 'twere, the mirror up to nature; to show virtue her own feature, scorn her own image, and the very age and body of the time his form and pressure. Now this overdone or come tardy off, though it make the unskillful laugh, cannot but make the judicious grieve; the censure of the which one must in your allowance o'erweigh a whole theatre of others. O, there be players that I have seen play, and heard others praise, and that highly not to speak it profanely, that neither having the accent of Christians nor the gait of Christian, pagan, nor man, have so strutted and bellowed, that I have thought some of nature's journeymen had made men, and not made them well, they imitated humanity so abominably.

FIRST PLAYER: I hope we have reformed that indifferently with us, sir.

HAMLET: O, reform it altogether. And let those that play your clowns speak no more than is set down for them: for there be of them that will themselves laugh, to set on some quantity of barren spectators to laugh to, though in the mean time some necessary question of the play be then to be considered: that's villanous, and shows a most pitiful ambition in the fool that uses it. Go, make you ready.

Exeunt PLAYERS

(Speech taken from *Shakespeare: The Complete Works,* published by Michael O'Mara, Books Limited.)

ACKNOWLEDGMENTS

Everyone should have somebody in their lives who champions them. I have been fortunate enough to have many such people:

From left to right: My daughter, Marian; my wife, Elaine; me; and my son, David. *Photo by Chris Jurgenson.*

Miss Steigman, my grammar school teacher, for reading *Julius Caesar* to me after school, and for casting me in our many school plays

Herbert Ratner, Harold Clurman, Joe Bromberg, and Morris Carnovsky are the finest artists and teachers with which I have had the privilege of working. Betty Geffen, my beloved manager who rekindled my career from the blacklist

John Crosby, my friend of thirty years, for opening doors for me wherever and whenever he could

My thanks go out to Joe D'Agosta, who cast me in *Baretta* in 1975, my first job after moving to Los Angeles. And director Boris Sagal, who cast me in my first Movie of the Week and introduced me to Lila Garrett.

And thanks to Lila Garrett, a three-time Emmy-winning writer and director, for hiring me over and over again.

I want to thank the many movie directors who have hired me over the years. This list includes Sidney Lumet, Karel Reisz, Barry Levinson, Robert Redford, Robert Aldrich, Irwin Winkler, Graham Clifford, Richard Serafian, Ron Maxwell, Alan Alda, Michael Schroeder, Martha Coolidge, Jerry London, and Francis Ford Coppola. Special thanks to my dear friend Arthur Friedman, who was responsible for getting me auditions for *Quiz Show* and *Disclosure.*

Me and my pals Buddy Hackett and Arthur Friedman at the Pritikin Center, where we were losing weight.

I also want to thank the many generous actors I've worked with over the years who have given me great support and inspiration, many of whom are no longer with us: Claude Rains, Edward G. Robinson, Henry Fonda, Lucille Ball, Lee J. Cobb, Chester Morris, Glen Anders, Whitford Kane, Ivan Simpson, Alexander Scourby, Cliff Dunstan, Mike Kellin, Mike Strong, Jeannie Cagney, and many other fine actors.

World-renowned artist Sid Maurer.

I would like to thank Scott Sanders, the archivist at Antioch College, for providing all the Axel Bahnsen photos of those early years (1946 to 1952) with the Area Theater in Ye Old Opera House and the Shakespeare Repertory in 1952.

To all the hard-working agents and casting directors who fought on my behalf and helped in convincing the powers-that-be to hire me. I am all too aware that without their help I would be among those many actors who rarely ever work.

To Sid Maurer, my friend for over seventy-four years, I thank you. His painting of me graces the cover of this book. His other works are peppered throughout the book. He is a great and prolific artist.

To all of my students, past, present, and future: those wonderful young people who struggle to become actors. Bravo! So, to all of you: stars, feature players, commercial actors, those of you on soaps and series, and of course, those of you who were smart enough to leave this madness to make families and live normal lives—I thank you all for helping me share whatever I've learned.

Thanks to Howard Preiser for his insightful and invaluable editorial eye. He insisted on a new level of clarity and meaning in the many sections we worked on together. The book was exponentially improved as a result of his help.

A very special thanks to actress Frances Fisher for the wonderful work she did with me in *My Sexiest Year* in May of 2006.

Last, but not least, many thanks to my incredible assistant and good friend, David Rickett. He allowed me to bounce ideas off him repeatedly, keeping me in line with my purpose. His additions and deletions were immense help in writing a book intended to help my fellow actors.

Actress Frances Fisher and me at a Miami sushi bar after working on *My Sexiest Year. Photo by David Rickett.*

SPECIAL THANKS*

David Adnopoz

Zoe Adnopoz

Maria Conchita Alonso

Dan Amernick

Jay Amernick

Curtis Armstrong

Angela Arthur

Irvin Atkins

James Avery

Burke Bryant

Nancy Cassaro

Larry Cord

Chris Coronado

Ed Cotter

John Crosby

Richard D'Abo

Omar Daher

Isabelle Dahlin

Don Davis

Jon Davis

Brian Dee

Robert DoQui

Fran Drescher

Randy English

Jesse Erwin

Sam Espinoza

John Farrand

Fotokem

Arthur Freidman

Matt Gerson

Nancy Giacomi

Kari Gibson

Grant Gilmore

Dean Goodhill

Cuba Gooding Jr.

Eric J. Goldstein

Gary Gossett

Michael Greyeyes

Marcia Groff

Jeffery R. Gund

Carol Gustafson

Terry Hagerty

Dru & Michael Hammer

Mariska Hargitay

Jed Hathaway

Melissa Havard

Whit Haydn

Kia Hellman

Thomas Hildreth

Vanessa Hopkins

Cheryl & Jackie Jacobs

Chris Jurgenson

Amy Holden Jones

Douglas Kaback

Steve Kurzfeld

Judith Ledford

Twyla Littleton

Tre Lovell

Karen Martin-Messner

Masquers Cabaret

Debi Mazar

Joe McCullough

Morgan Mead

Russell Means

Nick Nitti

Zack Norman

Panavision

Bruce Payne

Linda Porter

---

*As you can see, you don't make it alone. My apologies to those who belong on this list but were not included.

Willard E. Pugh

Bert Ramos

Philip Roth

Scott Sanders

William & C. L. Scott

Screen Actors Guild

Michael Shapiro

Harris Smith

Patrick Smith

Howard Taksen

Sven-Ole Thorsen

Toys "R" Us

Gloria Villa

Jerry & Liz Ward

Jeffrey S. Wigand

Wilshire Stages

Madeline Zima

APPENDIX
GREAT PERFORMANCES

The following is a list of films containing at least one great performance. After watching these amazing performances, go back to the Five Focuses and see if you can apply your new knowledge. Were these performances convincing? Can you now figure out why and how? Write a paper on each performance and share it with your fellow actors.

A Double Life

A Face in the Crowd

A Night at the Opera

A Streetcar Named Desire

All About Eve

All Quiet on the Western Front

Amadeus

Barry Lyndon

Being There

The Bicycle Thief

The Big Night

Birdman of Alcatraz

Bob & Carol & Ted & Alice

Body and Soul (1947)

Bonnie and Clyde

Born Yesterday

The Bridge on the River Kwai

Brute Force (1947)

The Caine Mutiny

Camille (1936)

Casablanca

Champion (1949)

Chinatown

Citizen Kane

City Lights

Counselor at Law

The Deer Hunter

The Devils (1971)

Dinner at Eight

Disraeli

Doctor Zhivago

Dodsworth

Double Indemnity

Dr. Ehrlich's Magic Bullet

Dr. Strangelove or: How I Learned to Stop Worrying and Love the Bomb

Duck Soup

E.T. the Extra-Terrestrial

East of Eden

The Elephant Man

Elizabeth the Queen

The Entertainer

Executive Suite (1954)

Fanny & Alexander

The Four Hundred Blows

Frances

The French Connection

Full Metal Jacket

Funny Girl

The Gambler

The Godfather

The Godfather, Part II

Gone with the Wind

The Good Earth

Grand Hotel

The Great Ziegfeld

Guess Who's Coming To Dinner

Hamlet

The Heiress

Henry V

His Girl Friday

The House of Rothschild

Hush . . . Hush Sweet Charlotte

The Hustler (1961)

Il Postino

It's a Wonderful Life

Jane Eyre

Jezebel

Joe

The Killers

Kind Hearts and Coronets

King Kong (1933)

Kramer vs. Kramer

La Dolce vita

La Strada

Lady Sings the Blues

Last Exit to Brooklyn

Last Tango in Paris

Lawrence of Arabia

Les Miserables

The Lion in Winter

Little Odessa

Lost Horizon

Lust for Life

The Man in the White Suit

The Manchurian Candidate (1962)

Marathon Man

Miller's Crossing

Moscow on the Hudson

Moulin Rouge

Mr. Smith Goes to Washington

Ninotchka (1939)

Notorious

The Old Man and the Sea

On the Waterfront

Open City

Othello (1995)

Panic in the Streets

Paths of Glory

Patton

The Pawnbroker

Pinocchio (1940)

Psycho (1960)

Quiz Show

Raging Bull

Rashomon

Rebel Without a Cause

Red River

Reds

The Roaring Twenties

Rob Roy

Scarface (1932)

Scenes from a Marriage

Schindler's List

Serpico

Seven Beauties

Seven Year Itch

The Shop Around the Corner

Singin' in the Rain

Single White Female

The Snake Pit

Some Like It Hot

Sophie's Choice

Stagecoach (1939)

The Stranger (1946)

Suddenly Last Summer

Sweet Smell of Success

Taxi Driver

To Be or Not to Be

To Kill a Mockingbird

Tootsie

Topper (1937)

Touch of Evil

Twelve Angry Men

Unforgiven

Viva Zapata!

What Ever Happened to Baby Jane?

White Heat (1949)

Wild Strawberries

Witness for the Prosecution

The Wizard of Oz

Women in Love

Wuthering Heights

Yankee Doodle Dandy

Zeffirelli's *Romeo and Juliet*

Zorba the Greek aka *Alexis Zorbas*

INDEX

CPSIA information can be obtained at www.ICGtesting.com
Printed in the USA
LVOW020949100112

263086LV00001B/6/A